THE TH ̣ ISRAEL

Rabbi Eliyahu Avichail

THE TRIBES OF ISRAEL

Translated from Hebrew by Stepanie Nakache
Edited by Sarah Edri

Jerusalem 5765

Amishav
POB 6712
Efrat, Israel 90435

Copyright © 2012 by: Rabbi Eliyahu Avichail
All rights reserved.

ISBN: 1-4782-1440-6
ISBN-13: 9781478214403

CONTENTS

Seekers of Judaism in the World

PREFACE

Many books have been written about the Lost Tribes of Israel and their fate. Comprehensive material exists on numerous groups around the world that are in some way linked to the Jewish people. However, in the past, most of the works dealing with practical material were placed in the category of folklore. Much of the material was based on hearsay evidence which could not be investigated or proved, and was therefore not treated seriously by the scientific community. Although it is difficult to ascertain the veracity of the information today, the literature remains important, principally because of the opinions of the great Torah scholars in the matter.

The aim of this book is to engage a new discussion on the subject of the Ten Tribes, corresponding in as far as possible to current reality, and without relation to past hearsay evidence. The book has two main objectives: firstly, to present a general picture to the reader of how the subject is reflected in the Bible, in the writings of our Sages, and in the responsa of Torah luminaries through the generations; and secondly, to present the most recent information on the tribes and groups that possess many traditions apparently linking them to the Jewish People. It also relates the attitude of religious leaders today towards these various groups and to the work of the Amishav organization, and presents accounts of some of the expeditions of Amishav emissaries to the various groups. The report on these expeditions constitutes the practical side of the work.

This book constitutes a sequel to "The Lost Tribes of Assyria", which described the activities of Amishav since its founding, and presented a description of the different tribes and their relationship to the Jewish people. This volume contains both additional factual material and a discussion of the scholastic and philosophical aspects of the subject. It should be noted that the material presented here on each tribe, and also the theoretical material, was selected from a wealth of data collected by the Amishav organization.

The book is titled "The Tribes of Israel", because it includes information not only on the Lost Ten Tribes, but also on various other groups which are related genealogically to the tribe of Judah, and which must be reintegrated in the Jewish People. I have totally dedicated myself to this enterprise since 1960.

Amishav, the Organization on Behalf of the Dispersed of Israel, was founded in 1975 with the encouragement of Rabbi Zevi Yehuda Kook, of blessed memory, the head of the "Merkaz Harav" Yeshiva in Jerusalem and the spiritual leader of Religious Zionist Judaism. Rabbi Kook supported Amishav and encouraged its various activities to his last days.

The objectives of the Amishav organization have remained constant since its inception, being both the scientific research of the Lost Tribes of Israel, and the actual ingathering of these lost people, first back to Judaism, and then to the Jewish People and to the Land of Israel.

The activities of Amishav continue today under the guidance of the spiritual leaders of Israel, who encourage the organization to act in all matters pertaining to the physical redemption of Israel as manifested in the ingathering of the Lost Tribes. Amishav has brought about the dissemination of information on this subject, both in Israel and the Diaspora; an increase in activists engaged in this task; a large-scale awakening to their Jewish heritage among some of the Lost Tribes; and the actual return to Judaism, conversion and immigration to Israel of some of the lost people.

It is hoped that this important enterprise will be of interest to the entire Jewish people, particularly in light of the organization's success in Israel and throughout the world.

This book, like previous publications, is published by the Amishav Organization. This expanded and newly-translated edition in English contains corrections and additional information and photos. New editions have recently been published also in Hebrew and French.

I wish to thank all my colleagues in the Amishav organization who are active around the world: Acknowledgements are due also to our friend Dr. A. Moskovitz, our "Kulanu" friends in the Washington D.C. area, Mr. Gabriel Goldberg and family, and all of the organization's friends throughout the world who have assisted the organization since its founding. Special thanks to Mr. Alfonso Sabah, Adv. Menahem Kornweitz, Rabbi Arieh Kostiner, Mr. Micha Gross, Mr. Moshe Leshem, Mr. Yonatan Segal and Mr. Yehuda Amshalem.

My heartfelt thanks to Sarah Edri, who spent many hours rearding and editing the drafts of this edition.

Most of all, very special thanks to my wife Rivkah for her untiring efforts in hosting and guiding converts and proselytes of the various lost groups.

A blessing to them all

Rabbi Eliyahu Avichail

Jerusalem, 5765

ABOUT THE TEN TRIBES

Biblical Sources
Sources from the Talmud
Writings of the Great Sages

BIBLICAL SOURCES

And it came to pass at that time, when Jeroboam went out of Jerusalem, that the prophet Ahijah the Shilonite found him in the way; now Ahijah had clad himself with a new garment; and they two were alone in the field. And Ahijah laid hold of the new garment that was on him, and rent it in twelve pieces. And he said to Jeroboam: Take ten pieces; for thus says the Lord, the G-d of Israel; Behold, I will rend the kingdom out of the hands of Solomon, and will give **ten tribes** to you – but he shall have one tribe. (I Kings, 11:29-32)

Now the Lord said unto Ahijah: 'Behold, the wife of Jeroboam comes to inquire of you concerning her son; for he is sick; thus and thus shall you say to her: ... I will bring evil upon the house of Jeroboam... The Lord will raise Him up a king over Israel, who shall cut off the house of Jeroboam that day. But what is it even then? For the Lord will smite Israel, as a reed is shaken in the water; and He will root up Israel out of this good land, which He gave to their fathers, and will scatter them beyond the River...' (I Kings, 14:5-15)

In the days of Pekah king of Israel, came Tiglath-Pileser king of Assyria, and took Ijon, and Abel-Beth-Maacah, and Janoah, and Kedesh, and Hazor, and Gilead, and Galilee, all the land of Naphtali; and he carried them captive to Assyria. (II Kings, 15:29)

In the twelfth year of Ahaz king of Judah began Hosea the son of Elah to reign in Samaria over Israel and reigned nine years. And he did that which was evil in the sight of the Lord, yet not as the kings of Israel that were before him. Against him came up Shalmaneser king of Assyria... Then the king of Assyria came up throughout all the land, and went up to Samaria, and besieged it three years. In the ninth year of Hosea the king of Assyria took Samaria, and carried Israel away to Assyria, and placed them in Halah and in Habor on the river Gozan, and in the cities of Medes. (II Kings, 17:1-6)

And it came to pass in the fourth year of King Hezekiah, which was the seventh year of Hosea son of Elah king of Israel, that Shalmaneser king of Assyria came up against Samaria and besieged it. And at the end of three years they took it; even in the sixth year of Hezekiah, which was the ninth year of Hosea king of Israel, Samaria was taken. And the king of Assyria carried Israel away to **Assyria, and put them in Halah and in Habor on the river of Gozan, and in the cities of Medes;** because they hearkened not to the voice of the Lord their G-d, but transgressed His covenant. (II Kings, 18:9-12)

And the children of the half-tribe of Manasseh dwelt in the land... And they broke faith with the G-d of their fathers and went astray after the gods of the peoples of the land, whom G-d destroyed before them. And the G-d of Israel stirred up the spirit of Pul king of Assyria, and the spirit of Tiglath-Pilneser king of Assyria, and he carried them away, even the Reubenites, and the Gadites and the half-tribe of Manasseh, and brought them to Halah, and Habor, and Hara, and to the river Gozan, unto this day. (I Chronicles, 5:23-26)

And it shall come to pass on that day, that the Lord will set His hand again the second time to recover the remnant of His people, that shall remain from Assyria, and from Egypt, and from Pathros, and from Cush, and from Elam, and from Shinar, and from Hamath, and from the islands of the sea. And He shall set up an ensign for the nations, and will assemble **the dispersed of Israel, and gather together the scattered of Judah** from the four corners of the earth. The envy also of Ephraim shall depart, and they that harass Judah shall be cut off; **Ephraim shall not envy Judah, and Judah shall not vex Ephraim.** But they shall fly upon the shoulders of the Philistines toward the west; together shall they spoil the children of the east; they shall lay their hands upon Edom and Moab; and the children of Ammon shall obey them. And the Lord will utterly destroy the tongue of the Egyptian sea; and with His scorching wind will

He shake His hand over the River, and will smite it into seven streams, and cause men to march over dry-shod. **And there shall be a highway for the remnant of His people, that shall remain from Assyria,** like as there was for Israel in the day that it came up out of the land of Egypt. (Isaiah 11:11-16)

And it shall come to pass in that day, that the Lord will beat off (His fruit) from the flood of the River unto the Brook of Egypt, and you shall be gathered one by one, O children of Israel. And it shall come to pass in that day, that a great horn shall be blown; and they shall come that were **lost in the land of Assyria,** and they that were dispersed in the land of Egypt; And they shall worship the Lord at the holy mountain in Jerusalem. (Isaiah 27: 12-13)

And he said: It is too light a thing that you should be My servant to raise up the tribes of Jacob and to restore the offspring of Israel; I will also give you for a light of the nations, that My salvation may be unto the end of the earth... Thus says the Lord: In an acceptable time have I answered you, and in a day of salvation have I helped you; and I will preserve you, and give you for a covenant of the people, to raise up the land, to cause to inherit the desolate heritages; Saying **to the prisoners: "Go Forth; to them that are in darkness: "Show yourselves";** ... Behold, these shall come from far; And, lo, these from the **north and from the west, and these from the land of Sinim.** (Isaiah 49)

Fear not, for I am with you; I will bring your seed from the east, and gather you from the west. I will say to the north: "Give up", and to the south: "Keep not back, bring My sons from far, and My daughters from the end of the earth." (Isaiah 43)

In those days **the house of Judah shall walk with the house of Israel, and they shall come together out of the land of the north** to the land that I have given for an inheritance to your fathers. (Jeremiah 3)

For, lo, the days come, says the Lord, that I will turn the captivity of **My people Israel** and Judah, says the Lord; And I will cause them to return to the land that I gave to their fathers, and they shall possess it... Therefore fear not, O Jacob my servant, says the Lord; neither be dismayed, O Israel; for, lo, I will save you from afar, and your seed from the land of their captivity; and Jacob shall again be quiet and at ease, and none shall make him afraid. (Jeremiah 30)

Thus says the Lord: A voice is heard in Ramah, lamentation, and bitter weeping, Rachel weeping for her children; She refuses to be comforted for her children, because they are not. Thus says the Lord: Refrain your voice from weeping, and your eyes from tears. For your work shall be rewarded, says the Lord; and they shall come back from the land of the enemy. And there is hope for your future, says the Lord, and your children shall return to their own land... Set yourself up waymarks; make guideposts; set your heart toward the highway, even the way which you went. Return O virgin of Israel; Return to these your cities. (Jeremiah 31)

Son of man, as for **your brethren, even your brethren, the men of your kindred,** and all the house of Israel, all of them, concerning whom the inhabitants of Jerusalem have said: Get you far from the Lord! Unto us is this land given for a possession; Therefore say: Thus says the Lord G-d: Although I have removed them far off among the nations, and although I have scattered them among the countries, yet have I been to them as a **little sanctuary** in the countries where they are come. Therefore say: Thus says the Lord G-d: I will even gather you from the peoples and assemble you out of the countries where you have scattered, and I will give you the land of Israel. And they shall come thither, and they shall take away all the detestable things thereof and all the abominations thereof. (Ezekiel 11)

Say to them: Thus says the Lord G-d: Behold, I will take the **children of Israel** from among the nations whither they are gone, and **will gather them** on every side, and bring them into their own land. And I will make them one nation in the land, upon the mountains of Israel. ... **And my servant David** shall be king over them, and they shall all have one shepherd. They shall also walk in My ordinances, and observe My statutes and do them. (Ezekiel 37)

Thus says the Lord G-d: This shall be the border, whereby you shall divide the land for inheritance according to **the twelve tribes of Israel,** Joseph receiving two portions. And you shall inherit it, one as well as another, concerning which I lifted up My hand to give it to your fathers. And this land shall fall unto you for inheritance... So shall you divide this land unto you according to the tribes of Israel. (Ezekiel 47)

Ephraim, **he mixes himself** with the people. (Hosea 7)

Woe to them that are at ease in Zion, and to them that are secure in the mountains of Samaria. ...That drink wine in bowls and anoint themselves with the chief ointments; **But they are not grieved for the hurt of Joseph.** Therefore now shall they go captive at the head of them that go captive. (Amos 6)

And the house of Jacob shall be a fire, and the **house of Joseph** a flame, and the house of Esau for stubble, and they shall kindle in them and devour them; And there shall not be any remaining of the house of Esau for the Lord has spoken. (Obadiah)

In that day, says the Lord, will I assemble her that is lame, and I will gather her that is driven away, and her that I have afflicted. And I will make her that was lame a remnant, and her that was cast off a mighty nation; and the Lord shall reign over them in mount Zion... (Micah 4)

For then will I turn to the people a pure language that they may all call upon the name of the Lord, to serve Him with one consent. **From beyond the rivers of Ethiopia** shall they bring my supplicants, even the daughter of my dispersed, as my offering... I will deal with all them that afflict you; and **I will save her that is lame and gather her that was driven away.** And I will make them to be a praise and a name, whose shame has been in all the earth. (Zephaniah 3)

Thus says the Lord of Hosts: Behold, I will save my people from the east country, and from the west country; and I will bring them, and they shall dwell in the midst of Jerusalem. And they shall be My people, and I will be their G-d in truth and in righteousness. (Zechariah 8)

And I will strengthen the house of Judah, **and I will save the house of Joseph** and I will bring them back, for I have compassion upon them, and they shall be as though I had not cast them off; For I am the Lord their G-d, and I will hear them. And they of Ephraim shall be like a mighty man, and their heart shall rejoice as through wine; their children shall see it and rejoice, their heart shall be glad in the Lord. **I will hiss for them, and gather them,** for I have redeemed them; for they shall increase as they have increased. And I will sow them among the people and they shall remember me in far countries; and they shall live with their children, and shall return.

I will bring them back also out of the land of Egypt and gather them out of Assyria; **And I will bring them into the land of Gilead and Lebanon, and place shall not suffice them.** (Zechariah 10)

G-d spoke in His holiness that I would exult, that I would divide Shechem, and mete out the valley of Succoth. Gilead is mine, and Manasseh is mine, Ephraim also is the strength of my head, Judah is my scepter. (Psalms 60)

Josiah was eight years old when he began to reign... Now in the eighteenth year of his reign... He sent... to repair the house of the Lord his G-d. And they came to Hilkiah the high priest and delivered the money that was brought into the house of G-d, which the Levites, the keepers of the door, had gathered **of the hand of Manasseh and Ephraim, and of all the remnant of Israel, and of all Judah and Benjamin, and they returned to Jerusalem.** And they delivered it into the hand of the workmen that had the oversight of the house of the Lord. (Chronicles II, 34)

And Josiah kept a Passover unto the Lord in Jerusalem... And there was no Passover like that kept in Israel from the days of Samuel the Prophet; Neither did any of the kings of Israel keep such a Passover as Josiah kept, and the priests, and the Levites, and all Judah **and Israel that were present,** and the inhabitants of Jerusalem. (Chronicles II, 35)

SOURCES FROM THE TALMUD

"And you shall be lost among the nations" (Leviticus 26). R. Akiva says: "These are the Ten Tribes which were exiled to Media". Others say: "And you shall be lost" is an exile and not destruction, because it is also stated "And the land of your enemies shall devour you", and this is annihilation, but dispersal among the nations is an exile and not annihilation. (Sifra, Behukotai 8)

"And you shall perish quickly" (Deuteronomy 11) – exile following exile. Just as with the Ten Tribes you find exile following exile, so also you find this with the tribes of Judah and Benjamin. (Sifrei, Ekev 11:17)

"And he said, behold, I make a covenant" – and where is the covenant fulfilled – when they will be captives on the rivers of Babylon, **and I will remove them from there and place them within the boundary of the Sambatyon river,** and these are the "marvels such as have not been done in all the earth". (Targum Jonathan, Exodus 34, 10)

How do we know that mourners are obligated to perform loving-kindness? We learn it from the people of Yavesh Gilead who, when King Saul and his sons were killed, said: "Are we not obligated to perform loving-kindness to the man who saved us from Bnei Ammon?" And their valiant men traveled all night to the walls of Beth Shean, as is stated: "All the valiant men arose, and went all night, and took the body of Saul" (Samuel I, 31). Said the Lord, I will repay them at the time when I gather Israel from the four corners of the earth, first will the half-tribe of Manasseh be gathered, as it says: "Gilead is mine, and Manasseh is mine" (Psalms 60), and after that Ephraim will be gathered, as it says: "Ephraim also is the strength of my head, Judah is my scepter". (Pirkei de-Rabbi Eliezer 17, Yalkut Shimoni, Psalms 60)

Menahem Ben Amiel said: the son of Joseph will have the greatest horns with which it will gore the four corners of the world. About him

Moses said: "The firstling of his herd, grandeur is his, and his horns are the horns of a wild ox, – and with him are the ten thousands of Ephraim, and they are the thousands of Manasseh". (Deuteronomy 33) (Ibid., chap. 19)

R. Abba Bar Kahana said: The Ten Tribes were not treated like the generation of the Deluge. About the generation of the Deluge it is written, "all the impulse of the thoughts of his heart was only evil continually" (Genesis 6). About the Ten Tribes it is written: "Woe to them that devise iniquity, and work evil upon their beds!" (Micah 2); which is at night. And also during the day it is said: "When the morning is light, they execute it" (ibid.). Of the generation of the Deluge not a remnant survived; should there be a remnant of these? **Yes, because of the merit of the righteous men and women who will be their offspring.** (Bereshit Rabba 28)

R. Yehuda heard from R. Hanin who said in the name of R. Shmuel son of Isaac: The exile originated with the drunkenness of Noah. The Ten Tribes were exiled because of wine, as it is written: "Woe to them that rise up early in the morning, that they may follow strong drink" (Isaiah 5). **The tribes of Judah and Benjamin were exiled because of wine,** as it is said: "But they also reel through wine" (Ibid. 28). (Bereshit Rabba 36, 7)

R. Yehuda son of Simon said that the Ten Tribes were exiled to a different place than the tribes of Judah and Benjamin. The Ten Tribes were exiled to within the Sambatyon River, while the tribes of Judah and Benjamin are scattered throughout the lands. (Bereshit Rabba 73, 5)

R. Yoshia Ben Levi resolved verses dealing with the exiles thus: "And G-d Almighty give you mercy before the man" (Genesis 48). The man is G-d, as it says: "The Lord is Man of War, the Lord is His Name" (Exodus 15). "That He may release to you your brother" (Genesis 48), these are the Ten Tribes, "The other and Benjamin" (ibid.), these are the tribes of Judah and Benjamin. (Bereshit Rabba 92, 3)

There are twelve constellations in the heaven. And just as the heavens cannot exist without the twelve constellations, so the earth cannot exist without the Twelve Tribes. (Shmot Rabba 15, 7)

"And he that smites his father" (Exodus 21) – And who did that? The Ten Tribes who refused to accept the yoke of G-d causing Sanneherib to exile them. The allegory is of a king who had ten sons who rebelled against him, and revoked his ten epigrams. Said he – "as you revoked that which is mine, I will send a fly to avenge me". Similarly, the Ten Tribes rebelled against G-d and did not fulfill the Torah, as is written: "They have belied the Lord and said; it is not He" (Jeremiah 5), so He sent the fly upon them, as it is written: "The Lord shall whistle to the fly" (Isaiah 7), which is Sanneherib. Therefore, nullifying the commandments is likened to cursing father and mother. (Shmot Rabba 30, 5)

"Now therefore, O children, hearken unto me – remove your way far from her – lest you give your vigor unto others" (Proverbs 5). What is "Now therefore, O children, hearken unto me"? He means the Ten Tribes and the tribes of Judah and Benjamin for **all children were called "sons"**, as is written "You are the children of the Lord your G-d" (Deuteronomy 14). "Lest you give your vigor unto others" – That they were exiled from their land and strangers occupied their place and devoured all their efforts. And you find that when the king of Assyria exiled the Ten Tribes he settled strangers in their land, as is written: "And the king of Assyria brought men from Babylon, and from Cuthah and from Avva and from Hamath" (Kings II, 17). **All this happened to the Ten Tribes, and their fate was sealed, for committing adultery,** as is written "That lie upon beds of ivory, and stretch themselves upon their couches" (Amos 6). (Bamidbar Rabba 9, 4)

The tribe of Judah, its wise men and important leaders, had a tradition from Jacob our Forefather, describing all that will befall each of the tribes until the coming of the Messiah. And each of the tribes had a tradition as to what will befall them until the coming of the Messiah. (Bamidbar Rabba 13, 13)

"I am black" (Song of Songs 1) describes the Ten Tribes, "But comely" (ibid.) describes the tribe of Judah and Benjamin. (Song of Songs Rabba, 1, 2)

"Your eyes are as doves (Song of Songs 4). Just as a dove migrates and returns to its roost, so does Israel. As is written "As a dove from Assyria" (Hosea 11). Those are the Ten Tribes, and both "Will be resettled in their homes, says G-d". (Song of Songs Rabba 4)

They were exiled in groups. R. Eliezer says: "The tribes of Reuven and Gad were exiled first". R. Shimon Ben Gamliel says: "The tribes of Zevulun and Naphtali were exiled first". It is written (Isaiah 8): "Now the first made light of the land of Zevulun and the land of Naphtali". And how does R. Eliezer interpret the saying of Rabbi Shimon Ben Gamliel? "Now" that Reuven and Gad were exiled, so were exiled also Zevulun and Naphtali. (Ptihta D'Aikha Rabba 5)

R. Hanina and R. Yonatan both say: What were the Ten Tribes on one side and the tribes of Judah and Benjamin on the other side like? They were like two people wearing a new garment in the winter, each tugging on their side until they tore the garment. In the same way, the Ten Tribes were worshipping idols in Samaria, and the tribe of Judah was worshipping idols in Jerusalem, causing the destruction of Jerusalem. (Ptihta D'Aikha Rabba 12)

R. Akiva says: "Widow" (Lamentations 1) and you say "As a widow"? Rather a widow from the Ten Tribes and not from the tribes of Judah and Benjamin. And the Sages say – a widow from both, but not from G-d, as is written "Israel is not a widower, nor Judah from his G-d" (Jeremiah 51). (Lamentations Rabba 1,3)

What did the Ten Tribes do? They sent oil to Egypt to buy their support, and wheat to Babylon to buy their help, so that if enemies come, these nations will help. As is written, "They made a covenant with Assyria and transported oil to Egypt" (Hosea 12) (Lamentations Rabba 4,20)

The Ten Tribes were exiled and none survived. The tribes of Judah and Benjamin were exiled, and survived. (Ecclesiastes Rabba 5,1)

R. Levi said: Sanneherib caused three exiles. First he exiled the tribes of Reuven and Gad, secondly the Ten Tribes, and third was Judah. (Ecclesiastes Rabba 9,27)

The Ten Tribes were exiled because of wine. See what is written: "Woe to them that are at ease in Zion, and to them that are secure in the mountain of Samaria – that drink wine in bowls" (Amos 6) (Tanhuma, Shmini 5)

The Temple will be built before the ingathering of the Diaspora. The ingathering of the Diaspora will take place before the resurrection of the dead. And the resurrection of the dead will be last in occurring. Where is the proof of this? It is written, "G-d builds Jerusalem and gathers the dispersed of Israel". "Who heals the broken in heart and binds up their wounds" (Psalms 147). And this is the resurrection of the dead. (Midrash ha-Ne'lam [Zohar], Toledot 130)

Moses said: "And you will perish among the nations" (Leviticus 26). Isaiah came and nullified this decree, as it is written: "And on that day a great horn shall be blown and those that were lost in the Land of Assyria shall come" (Isaiah 27) (Yalkut Shimoni, Part I, 291)

"In the twentieth year of Pekah **came Tiglath-Pileser** king of Assyria, and took Ijon" and took the two golden calves and smashed them and departed – Ahaz king of Judah and Hosea son of Elah were enslaved to the king of Assyria for eight years. In the twelfth year (of Pekah's reign) [of Ahaz's reign] G-d stirred up the spirit of Pul king of Assyria and he exiled the tribes of Reuben and Gad and he took the calf which was in Beth-El and departed. ... When Hosea son of Elah saw that the golden calves were exiled he removed the guards stationed by Jeroboam son of Nabet to prevent pilgrimages to Jerusalem. ... This is when **Shalmaneser** the king of Assyria approached. ... When Hosea son of Elah saw that the king of Assyria was preparing to exile Israel for a third time, he made an alliance with the kings of Egypt – as it is written: "And the king of Assyria found that Hosea plotted by sending messengers to So king of Egypt" (Kings II, 17). "In the fourth year of Hezekiah **Shalmaneser** came up to Samaria and besieged it". In the sixth year of Hezekiah's reign, which was the ninth year of Hosea's rebellion, Samaria was captured – "And the king of Assyria carried Israel away into Assyria". As it is written: "And the Lord rooted them out of their land" (Deuteronomy 29). **There were eight years between the first Exile and the second Exile, and another eight years between the second Exile and the third Exile.** (Yalkut Shimoni II, 236)

"And these are from the north and the west" – those who are very far. "Those from the land of Sinim" – these are the descendents of Yonadav Ben Rechav. (Yalkut Shimoni II, 469)

"There they are in great fear" (Psalms 14), and in another place is written: "There was no fear" (ibid). "There are they in great fear" are the Ten Tribes, "There was no fear" are the tribes of Judah and Benjamin. (Midrash Tehillim Shoher Tov Psalm 14)

"For the leader with string music – in Judah G-d is known, His name is great in Israel", as it is written: "Ephraim shall be desolate in the day of rebuke, among the tribes of Israel do I make known that which shall surely be" (Hosea 5). When the Ten Tribes were exiled and the tribes of Judah and Benjamin were not, the idol-worshipping nations of the world were saying that they were being favored, because they were guests in His house, and this is why He didn't exile them. But when they were exiled this was proof of G-d's sincerity in punishing them. (Ibid., Psalm 76)

Another explanation: "He gathers together the dispersed of Israel" (Psalms 147). These are the tribes. As it is written: "And cast them into another land" (Deuteronomy 29). And it is also written: "And they shall come that were lost in the land of Assyria" (Isaiah 27). And at this time Israel will be beyond pain, until they will be healed, as it is written: "Who heals the broken in heart". (Ibid., Psalms 147)

"And Reuven returned to the pit" (Genesis 37: 29). R. Eliezer, R. Joshua, and the Sages each have a different explanation as to from where he returned. R. Eliezer said that he returned from doing penance for his misdeed. R. Joshua said that it was his turn to care for the household. And the Sages said that G-d said to Reuven: You wanted to return a favored son to his father, therefore your grandchild will return Israel to their Heavenly Father. And this will be Hosea.

The word of the Lord that came unto Hosea son of Beeri" (Hosea 1, 1), and it is written: "Be'era his son, whom the king of Assyria carried away captive" (Chronicles I, 5-6). And why was he called Be'era? Because he was a wellspring of Torah. **And why did he die in exile? So that the Ten Tribes will repent.** (Pesikta de-Rav Kahana 24, 9)

In the days of Hosea son of Elah the king of Israel, the land was conquered, and in his days the Ten Tribes were exiled. But in what way were the deeds of Hosea such that Israel was exiled in his time? From the time of Jeroboam son of Nevat until Hosea son of Elah, idol worshipping was blamed on one man, and it was difficult for their Heavenly Father to exile the many of Israel for the sin of one man. But then came Hosea and removed the guards who guarded the roads and prevented the people from going to Jerusalem. He then announced that whoever wanted to go to Jerusalem could do so, and thereby **removed the blame from himself and placed it upon the multitudes.** Therefore it is written of him: "And he did that which was evil in the sight of the Lord, yet not as the kings of Israel that were before him. Against it came up Shalmaneser king of Assyria ... and carried Israel away" ... (Kings II, 17) (Tanna de-Vei Eliyahu ch. 9)

"Also our couch is leafy". These are the Ten Tribes that were exiled within the river Sambatyon, as it is written: "With the corner of couch" (Amos 3). That G-d saved but one of seven and one of eight. (Midrash Zuta, Song of Songs 1)

Following were the ten exiles of the dear sons of Zion: three exiles of Israel were by Sanneherib.

First exile: Sanneherib exiled the tribes of **Reuben, Gad and half of Manasseh.** "And he placed them in Halah, and Habor, on the river Gozan, and in the cities of the Medes" (Kings II, 17).

Second exile: Hosea son of Elah was enslaved by Sanneherib for eight years, and after eight years Sanneherib came and exiled **the tribes of Zevulun and Naphtali,** as it is written: "For is there no gloom to her that was steadfast? Now that the former has lightly afflicted the lands of Zevulun and Naphtali, but the latter has dealt a more grievous blow by the way of the sea, beyond the Jordan in the district of the nations" (Isaiah 8), from which we learn that he had no respect for the two tribes.

Third exile: This is the exile of Samaria. Sanneherib brought Kutiim from Babylon and from Hamat and from Aviim and from Sfarviim, and they settled in Samaria, at first under the rule of Israel, and later they took over Samaria until Sanneherib returned and exiled them.

Seventh exile: This is the exile of the Ten Tribes, who were exiled to within the River Sabbatyon. **And why was it called Sabbatyon? Because it rested on the Sabbath.** When Israel were led captives to Babylon, evil Nebuchadnezzar said to them: Come and sing praises before my idol as you do before your G-d. Then each of Israel inserted a finger into their mouth and cut their tongues with a knife so that they would not be forced to sing praises before an idol. **Therefore G-d covered them in clouds of glory, removed them, and placed them past the river Sabbatyon,** as it is written: "I will make mention of Rahab" (Psalms 87). (Midrash Eser Galuyyot [Ten Exiles], Eisenstein: Otzar Midrashim, p. 435)

It happened that Mar Jacob son of Eliezer traveled in the land of Khazaria, and he saw there the tribe of Shimon, and he said: Woe to us that saw the fulfillment of that which was written: "And you will I scatter among the nations" (Leviticus 26). And when he later saw a Khazar who had converted to Judaism he quoted "and yet for all that, when they are in the land of their enemies, I will not reject them" (Ibid.)

Jerusalem was exiled ten times. **Four times by Sanneherib,** four times by Nebuchadnezzar, once by Titus, and once by Adrianus. **First time:**

Sanneherib came and exiled Reuven, Gad and half of Manasseh and took the golden calves which were made by Jeroboam son of Nevat. It was these calves which the sons of Reuven and Gad and half of the tribe of Manasseh brought from Dan, and built a temple for them, and for which they were removed from their land and placed in a different land to this day. When Sanneherib came, removed them, and placed them in Lahlah, Habor, the river Gozan and the cities of Medes, the king of Israel was Pekah son of Remaliahu. When Hosea son of Elah saw that the soldiers of Pekah were so diminished in number, he killed Pekah and became king of Israel, reigning in Samaria five years, and this was the first exile.

Sanneherib heard of this, laid siege to Hosea son of Elah, who brought tribute, **and then exiled the tribes of Asher, Zevulun, Naphtali and Issachar,** who did not accept Hosea son of Elah as king. He then appointed Hosea son of Elah over Samaria – so that Hosea was king over Israel and Judah – and this was the second exile.

When Ahaz died, Hezekiah his son became king. At the beginning of the fourth year of his reign, Sanneherib returned to Samaria, laid siege for three years, and in the seventh year of the reign of Hezekiah he exiled from Samaria **the tribes of Ephraim and Manasseh – and this was the third exile.**

Eight years later Sanneherib arrived again with men from Babylon, Kush, Avi, Hamat and Safarvi, and laid siege upon the fortified cities of Judah. Judah had a hundred and fifty cities inhabited by the tribes of Judah and Shimon, and Sanneherib conquered them and planned to remove them to Lahlah to join the other tribes. But then he heard that the king of Kush had rebelled against him, and since the land of Kush was on the other side of Egypt, **he took the tribes of Judah and Shimon with him, and in a miraculous way they arrived to behind the mountains of darkness which are past the rivers of Kush. And this was the fourth exile by Sanneherib.** (Ektan D'Mar Yakov, Otzar Midrashim, pp. 436-7)

And he also told us, that when the Temple was destroyed and Israel went to Babylon, the Chaldeans requested that the sons of Moses sing to them of the songs of Zion. And the sons of Moses stood crying before G-d, and damaged their fingers with their teeth, saying: The fingers that strummed in the Temple, how can they now strum in an impure land? **And a cloud covered them and carried them with their tents and sheep and cattle, and placed them at night in a place called Chavilla.** And he also told, that the forefathers tell that they heard a great noise at night, and in the morning they saw a great multitude surrounding them, separated by a river which flowed rocks and sand, in a place where there was no river before.

And this river still flows with rocks and sand, with great force and great thunder, capable of shattering a mountain of iron. And the river of rocks and sand flows with no water at all for six days, and it rests on the Sabbath. And on Friday evening a cloud comes to rest on the river, so that no one can approach the river until after the Sabbath. And the name of the river is Sambatyon, and we call it Sabbatino (or Sanbatyon). There are places where the river is no more than 60 cubits wide, so that we can converse with them on the other side, but they cannot be approached because the river surrounds them and we cannot cross to them, nor can they cross to us. (Eldad Hadani, First Story, Otzar Midrashim 20)

Only two tribes are scattered in Asia and Europe, and they suffer the yoke of Rome. But even now the Ten Tribes are on the other side of the Euphrates, uncounted thousands, and a nation of great multitudes. (Josephun, Book XI, chapter 8)

WRITINGS OF THE GREAT SAGES

Rabbi Abraham Ben David of Posquières (Rabad)
(c. 1125-1198 [4860-4958])

Rabbi Akiva explains: "And you shall be lost among the nations" – these are the Ten Tribes who were exiled to Medes.

Rabbi Akiva believed that the Ten Tribes will not return, and that their being lost is meant in a sense of complete annihilation. Others explain that this loss is exile. And still others say that even this exile is meant in a sense of annihilation, and that no one disputes R. Akiva's interpretation. And still there are those who say that **the loss refers to exile,** and even though it is written "And the land of the enemies shall devour them", it still does not imply annihilation. (Commentary on Leviticus 26)

Rabbi David Kimhi (Radak)
(1160-1235 [4907-4995])

"And on that day a great horn shall sound" – they will gather as if a great horn was sounded – those who were lost, who are the tribes which were exiled beyond the river where the king of Assyria placed them. **And this is the land of Assyria where they were so scattered as to seem that they will never return from there.** (Commentary on Isaiah 27)

Rabbi Moses ben Nahman (Nahmanides – Ramban)
(1194-1270 [4954-5030])

"I thought I would make an end to them" – in my opinion this is a complex word as mentioned in Sifri, but its meaning is that I will place them in an out of the way place, so that none will remain among the nations, and their location will not be known. (Sefer Hageula, p. 273, Schevel edition)

Rabbi Menahem Ben Solomon (HaMeiri)
(1249-1316 [5009-5076])

In the case of a gentile who marries in our day, we do not suspect him of being of Israel. For it was their tradition that the women who were exiled at that time made themselves so undesirable that no man wanted them. And it was also a tradition that **all those who assimilated, men and women, did so completely,** so that a Rabbinic court of that generation considered them gentiles, outside of the laws of Israel. (Beit Habehira to Yevamot 17,2)

Rabbi Levi Ben Gershon (Ralbag)
(1288-1344 [5048-5104])

"And will return and gather you from all the people" (Deuteronomy 30). This was not the Babylonian exile because the Ten Tribes that were exiled to Halah, Habor and the cities of Medes did not return, and so we are forced to understand that the Torah is hinting at our own exile.

(Commentary on the Torah, Vayelech) "And will return and gather you from all the peoples whither the Lord G-d has scattered you, if your dispersed are even in the uppermost parts of heaven" (Deuteronomy 30). This points to our own exile and to the ingathering of the Ten Tribes, because this did not take place yet, and we know this because during the Second Temple not all gathered, and most stayed under the yoke of other kingdoms. (Responsa, part 4, 187)

Rabbi Joseph Albo (Ha-Ikkarim)
(15th century [5140-5204])

It is clearly explained that many things prophesied by Ezekiel did not come to pass at the time of Ezra, nor during the Second Temple, such as the dividing of the land to the tribes, which did not happen during the Second Temple. (Fourth Treatise, 42)

Rabbi David Ben Zimra (Radbaz)

(1479-1573 [5240-5334])

Question – in chapter Helek – the Ten Tribes will not return, as R. Akiva says. And R. Eliezer disputes with him. We, however, must agree with R. Akiva, because we have established (Eruvin 40) that the Halakha is according to R. Akiva. So, accordingly, there will only be two tribes at the time of the Messiah. But our Sages have taught us the secret of the Twelve Tribes, so how is it possible that Ten Tribes will be absent, according to R. Akiva? In addition, it is written in Ezekiel 47: "Thus says the Lord G-d: This shall be the border whereby you shall divide the land..." Is this understood to be a prophecy for the future?

Answer: Know that there are those who explain that this dispute is not for the time of the Messiah, but for the World to Come. And so it seems from the baraita which is brought in the Talmud: "Our Sages learned that the Ten Tribes will not have a part in the World to come, as it is written: "And G-d scattered them..." – and so we can easily understand that what was meant is that the Ten Tribes alone were punished for being evil, but not their sons. However, many commentators agree that they will not return at the time of the Messiah, so we are compelled to explain that they were so evil that a Rabbinic court declared them complete gentiles, as it is written in Yevamot page 17, and so their sons, also, are not included in Israel, and we do not suspect their marriage as being a Jewish one. We can establish, however, that **there must have been a small number of people from other tribes in the land of Judah and Benjamin,** because important persons of all tribes resided in Jerusalem (Taanit 26). And when the time comes, each will come to know his family and tribe, and the few will increase, and each tribe will grow as the tribe of Benjamin did, until they will be as many as when they were in Egypt, as it is written: "I will make wonders as at the time when you came out of Egypt".

Not that I agree with the established explanation of what R. Akiva said, even with the first explanation, because two Tannaim disagree with him – R. Eliezer and R. Shimon Ben Yehuda of Akko in the name of R. Shimon. **And therefore I believe that they will return, and also have a part in the World to Come.** (Responsa, Orakh Haim p. 8, part 85)

Rabbi Tuviah ha-Levi (Hen Tov)
(5260?)

It seems to me that all explain the saying to both their credit and their discredit. "As of this day" – which is daylight returning after the night – or also as a day which once gone does not return. How can we explain it both ways? Gone without return for that specific generation, but shines again for their sons in the future. Even of those whom Jeremiah returned and over whom Josiah reigned, some returned and the day shone on them, and those who did not return will not return, as R. Akiva says. And R. Eliezer says that "this day" is for those who scattered, that their darkness will be brightened. (Nitzavim, page 301 – in commentary 6 Sanhedrin chap. 10)

Rabbi Azariah (Min HaAdummim) Rossi
(c. 1511-c. 1157 [5273-5338])

We find a discussion in the first chapter of Tractate Megillah that Josiah the king went to ask the advice of Hulda the Prophetess, and not of Jeremiah. About this R. Jochanan says that **Jeremiah had gone to fetch the Ten Tribes.**

You should not pay any attention to this deduction, **because it is a legend** that is not to be studied and accepted as tradition. We can, however, find in Chronicles II, 5, written by Ezra, as deduced in the first chapter of Tractate Baba Batra, that he writes about the exile of Halah and Habor, which was still in force in his day. **And if it was so in his day, certainly in the time of Josiah and Jeremiah they had not returned.**

In addition, if you claim that they returned, you make lies out of the prophecies that foretell of Judah and Israel dwelling together on their land, an event that had not yet taken place. In particular the prophecy of Ezekiel 37: "Take one wood for Judah and one wood for Ephraim", and the whole of the prophecy which is not conditional, but rather a vow by G-d to Judah – which is the kingdom of the two tribes, and to the whole of the house of Israel – which is the Ten Tribes. And we learnt a whole Mishna in chapter Helek about R. Akiva and R. Eliezer who lived during the

Destruction. We find them disputing the return of the tribes, from which we can deduce that in their time things had not changed.

Because of all these facts Rashi is forced to explain R. Jochanan's saying as meaning that Jeremiah went to fetch the tribes, but only few out of the many actually returned. (Me'or Einayim, part 3,13)

Rabbi Abraham Yagel (Beit Ya'ar Halevanon)
(5294?)

You see from these sayings that they are still in exile, and have not returned, though written in Tractate Megillah that Jeremiah fetched them. And we can interpret that statement as Rashi does in explaining R. Jochanan, that Jeremiah returned only few out of the many, and the rest were not so lost that they might be lost forever among the nations.

It is written: "I will not lose face to you for I am righteous and will not revenge for ever". This fits with the prophecy of Ezekiel about dividing the land equally among the Twelve Tribes, which implies that they will all return, each tribe with its people, so they can inherit equally. And it would be unfair that few of a tribe, as might have returned with Jeremiah, should divide equally with a fully peopled tribe. So we must say that they will inherit equally, although he meant the future generation, and not the evil generation that was exiled.

And about which is written of losing face because G-d is righteous, He means that you deserve My anger, but My righteousness will not allow an eternal anger about your sins, so after a long time of being angry their waiting will be rewarded by His returning among his people.

So this prophecy proves the return of the Ten Tribes, and that G-d will dwell within them forever, and they will no longer defile His Holy dwelling, so that these things are still to come to pass, including the dividing of the land of Israel to the Twelve Tribes. (The Shape of the Temple, Jerusalem 730)

Rabbi Samuel Eliezer ha-Levi Edels (Maharsha)
(1555-1631 [5315-5392])

Hosea prophesied that a ruler would rule over the Ten Tribes when they return. You may side with those who say at the end of Helek (p. 110) that the Ten Tribes will not return. But for those who say that the Ten Tribes will return, it is self understood that the ruler over the Ten Tribes when they return will be the Messiah, and may it be in our day, Amen. (Commentary on *Aggadot*, Arakhin 33)

We say then that **the Ten Tribes did not return in the days of Jeremiah**, but that Josiah went to various places in their tribal lands to destroy the idols that remained behind when they were exiled. (Ibid., Megillah 14)

Rabbi Moses Sofer Schreiber (Hatam Sofer)
(1762-1839 [5523-5600])

The redemption is one of the basic tenets of our faith, and if this tenet falls, then the whole wall will tumble down. Therefore I cannot believe that someone would say that our sins would cause us eternal exile, as does R. Akiva when he says that the Ten Tribes will be scattered forever.

However, since the basis of our faith is to believe in the Torah and the Prophets, and our final redemption is clearly stated there, then **whosoever doubts this final redemption denies the basic tenet of believing in the Torah and the Prophets.** (Responsa, Hatam Sofer Yoreh Deah, 356)

Rabbi Israel Lipschitz (Tiferet Yisrael)
(1782-1860 [5542-5620])

It seems to me that Jeremiah returned many of them, as indicated in Megilla and Arakhin, only that many who remained were assimilated into the gentiles. We knew that many of them were in India and China and Abyssinia, and they know only that they are Jews and they circumcise themselves and keep a few commandments. Their worship of G-d, however, is mixed with idol worship, and **on this point Rabbi Akiva and Rabbi Eliezer disagree: whether in the future those who were assimilated will return by force under the wings of the Divine Presence even though some of them are absolute idol worshippers, and they have even forgotten the name of Israel.** Only some Jewish customs remain from those of their ancestors, as in the case of the Afghan nation, whom some geographical scholars see as forgotten Jews. However, also in Egypt all were idol-worshippers and G-d in His mercy opened their eyes by force and redeemed them. (Commentary to Sanhedrin, Chapter Helek, Mishna 3)

Rabbi Zevi Hirsch Kalisher
(1795-1874 [5555-5635])

I remember with great regard the good which my friend has done within his people with regard to the Falashas, to encourage our brethren to undertake to teach those who are in error how to worship our G-d in accordance with the oral and written Torah, and how to avoid being trapped by the missionaries, G-d forbid.

It is certainly a great mitzvah. (From a letter to Rabbi Azriel Hildesheimer, published in the Book of the Jubilee, S. Carlebach, 1910)

Rabbi Azriel Hildesheimer
(1820-1899 [5580-5659])

Appeal to our brothers of Israel. For many years we have all been appalled by rumors coming from Africa, we have heard the cries of 250,000 of our brothers in the land of Kush (Abyssinia), who, because of the long exile and our sinfulness, retained only our 24 Holy Books, and Holidays, which were their reminders that they originated in Zion.

I know full well that each and everyone who hears of this terrible thing (that the missionaries are trying to entrap them) will be angry, because Israel are responsible for each other, and I, therefore, know that many of our faithful will make their concern known. And I, too, have not withheld my poor and weak hand, and have not rested, and have endeavored to speak up and express our thoughts in this matter, for my brothers and for G-d.

Therefore, be openhanded and generous in this important work for **our lost brothers in the Land of Abyssinia.** Do not weaken and be not silent, until this matter is settled, and the name of Israel will be glorified in the world.

Here in the Community of Eisenstadt, Hungary, 625. (In Hebrew, in the "Magid", year 5, edition 47)

Rabbi Abraham Isaac Hakohen Kook (RAI"H)

(1865-1935 [5625-5695])

(From the preface to the book "Kol Mevasser" of Rabbi S.K. Horowitz and from the book "Ma'amarei Hare'aya", part I)

Jerusalem 18 of Shvat 5673 (1913)

To my beloved friend, the great luminary, the repository of wisdom and master of the unrevealed, Rabbi Shimon Zevi Horowitz, Head of the Shaar HashamayimYeshiva, here in the holy city of Jerusalem, may it be built and remain forever.

I hereby expressly thank for your very valuable work in the precious book "Kol Mevasser", whose purpose is to arouse the interest of the best of our people to research and examine the whereabouts of our lost brothers classified in three general groups: **The Ten Tribes, the Rechabites, and the Sons of Moses.** You have compiled all that was written on this subject since ancient times, and all which concerns this holy matter, through the awakening of the spirit of purity in the hearts of Sages of Israel from past glorious generations to our very own generation. We witnessed great wonders when we saw how the idea of finding the Ten Tribes, which became so dear to the great man Menasseh Ben Israel of Blessed Memory, led to negotiations for the return of our brethren to Britain. And we see as a result of this deed the beginning of the redemption in our days, after the great events of the war, and the British declaration about our national home, which certainly was brought about by G-d. So that as a result of these events the general salvation will finally be revealed, which will bring closer the awaited redemption, with the help of G-d.

These three groups of brethren, who are hidden from us now and whom we so long to reveal, the Sons of Moses, the Ten Tribes and the Rechabites, are destined to be the surviving patrimony and the foundation for the reparation of the **three major losses** brought upon us by the exile and by the causes of the exile, namely the public and individual transgressions which preceded it, and which led our nation to this terrible crisis in which we find ourselves, "until the day breathes and the shadows flee away" (Song of Songs 2:17).

The first of the three losses **is the darkening of the light of the Torah,** because the exile of Israel from their place causes the greatest waste of the valuable time for learning Torah. (Tractate Hagiga, p. 5). This loss will be rectified by the Sons of Moses, the inheritors of the heavenly light of the Torah. "The depths of the Torah were given to Moses and his seed" (Tractate Nedarim, p. 35).

   The second loss is that of the failing of strength and spiritual might, which is a singular trait of Israel. "Torah was given to Israel because of their spiritual might" (Tractate Betza, p. 28). The exile removed this might, the Pride of Israel which was taken from them" (Tractate Hagiga, p. 5). This loss will be remedied through the influence of the **Ten Tribes;** we expect them to arrive as a complete group, upright, strong and proud, and with the undiminished might of Israel.

   The third loss is **the loss of integrity,** which was precipitated by the influence of the sinful nations that surrounded us. The causes of the exile and this bad influence, brought about by the foreign cultures of nations suffused with material desires, and the view of life and of the world which results from this suffusion, are the reason that we remain in the darkness of our exile until such time as the light of G-d will shine over us and a lowly nation will seek shelter in G-d's name. To repair the loss caused by these material influences will come the Sons of the **Rechabites,** those typical Nazirites who served as an example and beacon to all of Israel with their loyalty of spirit and in their keeping themselves from being washed away by the flow of material life at the time of the exile, as is explained in Jeremiah 35. Through them we will return to the healthy, humble and pure life, which should be natural to a holy nation on its holy land, chosen over all nations under the heavens. All these most precious qualities in the world – the light of the Torah which comes from an enriched and overflowing soul, the greatness of spirit made majestic by holiness, integrity, the quietness of life with spiritual contentment – **all are destined to return to us through the holiness of the Sabbath,** the source of blessings and the basis of the redemption, and the longing for the revelation of the Sambatyon (Tractate Sanhedrin p. 65; Bereshit Rabba 11:6), which represents a concept of the Sabbath as the supreme connection descending from the lights of holiness and revealing itself also in the activities of a world wallowing in its material nature. This expectation, may it come and be revealed to us speedily, is closely related to the preparation of the emergence of the light of redemption which will follow the revealing and ingathering of the three groups of our hidden brothers whom we long to see brought to us and united as brothers, and then together we will elevate the glory of the house of Israel in holy majesty with the might of G-d over His nation and His land.

Similarly, we must hope that your expectation, your research into this holy matter of seeking our hidden brothers, your travels and gathering of all which pertains to this glorious matter, will be productive with G-d's help, and will bring about a practical and spiritual awakening, and these matters will be clarified and elucidated in time, by the grace of the Rock of Israel.

I end this letter with the blessing that **we may merit to see in our time the speedy ingathering of our dispersed from the four corners of the earth, the house of Israel together with the house of Judah,** "Their king is passed before them, and the Lord at the head of them" (Micah 2:13), as the supplication of all prisoners of hope who are awaiting the redemption and salvation of the nation and land of G-d, the raising of the glory, and in the light of complete repentance, a repentance of love which will bring the redeemer to Zion speedily and in our lifetime, Amen.

Your loving friend .

Abraham Isaac HaKohen Kook

Rabbi Isaac Halevi Herzog

(1899-1959 [5659-5719])

(from a letter to the Jewish Agency, The Director of Torah Culture and Education in the Diaspora, Adar 29, 5714/1954)

I was extremely interested by the report you sent me. I congratulate you and wish you success in your effort to bring the Falashas closer to their Jewish origin, and there is great merit in this holy work. There is however, a very practical and interesting *Halakhic* point with regard to their marriage with Jews. The main question is whether they are descendants of converts or whether they are actually of the House of Israel. It is simpler if they are descendants of converts. The possibility of intermarriage which they mistakenly permitted, or divorces which certainly were not in accordance with the Torah, cause concern about the probability of *mamzerim* among them. This applies if they are of Jewish origin. However, if they are descended from gentiles who converted, then they converted in order to embrace a Judaism that is not our true Judaism, but rather a Judaism that they learned from their mentors. In this case, a lenient view may be taken and we may consider that according to Jewish law they are not Jews, and as a result, their marriages or divorces have no bearing on Judaism, and there is no longer a risk of *mamzerut*. Therefore, they need only undergo ritual immersion and then they will be permitted to marry Jewish women. Certainly, all the aforesaid is in the realm of conjecture, and must be properly investigated and clarified by the Chief Rabbinate of Israel... My impression is that researchers have concluded that the Ethiopians are of gentile stock who later converted.

May you find strength and courage to bring them into the Jewish fold, under the auspices of the Chief Rabbinate of Israel in Zion our home. Trust in the G-d of Israel, and endeavor to struggle against the missionaries who want the souls of our Ethiopian brethren, and may G-d strengthen and uphold you and us in our deeds.

With blessings of the Torah and the land,

Isaac Izik Halevi Herzog

Chief Rabbi of Israel

Rabbi Moses Feinstein

(1895-1986 [5655-5746])

(From a letter to his grandchild, Rabbi Mordechai Tendler, dated Sivan 26, 5744) Upon your request, I will hereby confirm what you wrote in my name a number of years ago regarding the "Falasha Jews". The Radbaz in his responsa (7:9) asserts that they are Jews; However, it is difficult to act upon his opinion halakhically, **because it is not certain that he was well acquainted with their situation**, nor that this situation has not changed from his time to ours. Halakhically, however, they are not *mamzerim*, though there are various other uncertainties.

Their Jewishness is uncertain, and they require true conversion before being permitted to enter the fold. However, even before their conversion they must be protected from the dangers that threaten to remove them from Israel, even if their Jewish origin is uncertain. **It must be understood that even if they are not Jews halakhically, their belief in their Jewishness and their willingness to die for this belief places an obligation on us to save them.**

As you mentioned, they should be brought to the land of Israel only after their conversion in order to prevent intermarriage. However, once they are properly converted, as I have heard that is done, they must be considered as other Jews and they must be upheld and supported in all their needs, both material and spiritual. We must prevent their being lost to the religion, which I think is done because of their dark color. They must be welcomed, but not because they are no less than other Jews, and *halakhically* their black color is not a hindrance, but also because they may be converts and we are commanded to love the convert.

I hope the situation will improve and the merit of fulfilling the commandments will hasten the ingathering of the Diaspora by our Messiah very soon.

Your loving grandfather,
Moshe Feinstein

Rabbi Ovadia Yosef

(from a letter to Mr. Aharon Cohen, 13 Adar I 5744/1988)

Please find below my answers to the questions you asked in your letter of Monday, Adar I 5744:

a. In the letter that I wrote on Friday 7 Adar I 5733 (1973) to Mr. Ovadia Hazzi, May the Lord watch over him, I based myself on the Radbaz and the Maharikas[1] that the Falashas are considered as Jews, that it is a religious precept to rescue them and to bring them to our Holy Land. In any case, when I saw that the Chief Rabbis who preceded me, including the Gaon Rabbi Isaac Halevi Herzog of blessed memory, established that

---

1 Rabbi Jacob Ben Abraham Castro, 1525-1610.

the Falashas should undergo a symbolic conversion by ritual immersion, without the necessity of a blessing for the women, and with only a ceremonial circumcision for the men, since they are already circumcised, I proceeded in accordance with this opinion. It may be that in some period the Falashas accepted converts into their community, and from ignorance of the laws of conversion, they were not converted properly in accordance with *Halakha*, and these converts intermarried into their community, and all the more so since in the book Otzar Israel (entry: Falashas), and in the responsa of Ziz Eleazar (part 12, para. 66), there is very great doubt as to their Jewishness. Therefore, in order to remove any doubt as regards their Jewishness, I instructed that the Falashas should undergo ritual conversion: for the men, a ceremonial conversion and immersion (without a blessing), and for the women, immersion (without a blessing) and for them to say that they assume the yoke of Torah and mitzvoth. (Like any convert who must assume the yoke of Torah and Mitzvoth ritually).

b. The measure of ritual conversion should never be abolished, based on the ruling of "Do not remove a precept instituted by your predecessors", since in this way the people would be divided into camps for purposes of marriage with the Falashas. Even though in any case the Radbaz is in doubt about the rabbinical marriages with Falashas, since they are not conversant with the nature of divorce and marriage, this is not developed sufficiently, but is more developed elsewhere (Jerusalem Talmud 86 Rosh Hashanah); in another place he answered at length on the question of admitting the Karaites also into the Jewish people, and the same applies to the Falashas. There is no more room here to enlarge on the subject.

c. After the Israeli government favorably received my provision of 1973, and we were fortunate that many Falasha Jews immigrated to Israel with their wives and children, it is a great mitzvah for all concerned to give them religious education. When they were in Ethiopia they were not acquainted with Jewish observance, and were very far from knowing the Oral Law. However, now that they are amongst us in our Holy Land, it is a sacred duty to teach them Torah, and to educate them to religious precepts and good deeds, in accordance with our Holy Torah, with wisdom and instruction to understand the words of wisdom in the laws of Shabbat and the Jewish holidays, *Kashrut*, and family purity, and the precepts of Eretz Israel and so forth, which if a man do, he shall live by them. And those who engage in this education have a great reward from the Holy One Blessed be He, as it is written: "if you bring forth the precious out of the vile, you shall be as my mouth". The Lord will reward their work and they will receive full remuneration from the Lord, when they do everything in their ability to return the dispersed of Israel to their origin and to restore passed glory.

Yours sincerely and with the blessing of the Torah, **Rabbi Ovadia Yosef**

THE TEN TRIBES

Exile and Redemption

Roots
Places of Exile
Legacy of the Exile
Return and Redemption

ROOTS

The Blessings

Before his death, Isaac our Patriarch wanted to bless his firstborn Esau with a material blessing: "So may G-d give you of the dew of heaven, and of the fatness of the earth".[1]

Rebecca, the loving mother, believed that Isaac was about to deliver to his son Esau the spiritual blessing, of which he was not worthy. This blessing was given by G-d to the Patriarchs: "Unto your seed will I give this land".[2] Rebecca, therefore, urged her younger son Jacob, the one who was learning Torah, to take this blessing for himself.

Jacob, obeying his mother, received from his father the material blessing, a fact that alarmed his father, who feared the effect of both blessings upon one man. Jacob was then forced to flee from his brother Esau, who wished to kill him. Before his departure, Jacob received also the spiritual blessing from his father: "And G-d Almighty bless you ... and give you the blessing of Abraham, to you, and to your seed with you, that you may inherit the land of your sojourning".[3] Jacob's act, which is to be considered an act of the Patriarchs that will be perpetuated throughout the generations by the descendants, **brings both a material and a spiritual blessing to Jacob and to the Jewish people.**

Rachel and Leah

Our Sages tell us that the younger Rachel was intended for the younger Jacob, while Leah, Laban's firstborn, was intended for Esau, the firstborn. Because of this Leah cried: "and Leah was tender eyed".[4] This division

1   Genesis 27:28.
2   Genesis 12:7.
3   Genesis 28:3-4.
4   Genesis 29:17.

corresponds to the original intent in Isaac's blessings which was to achieve a complementary relationship: Rachel, who represents the revealed material world, complements Jacob, the spiritual personality; Leah, who represents the hidden spiritual world, was intended to complement Esau, the material man. This original intent was disrupted by Rebecca, and Jacob, now in possession of both the material and spiritual blessings, **married both Rachel who was intended for him and Leah who was intended for Esau**. The way was thus prepared for a future separation of the people of Israel into two destinies and two kingdoms.

Joseph and Judah

Two kings rose to lead Israel: Judah the son of Leah, and Joseph the son of Rachel. The characteristics of these leaders are extensions of their mothers' basic traits: Judah is the leader in the **spiritual** realm, as it is written: "And he sent Judah before him, to show the way before him to Goshen". Our Sages interpret this as meaning that Judah was sent ahead to establish schools of learning for the tribes.[5] Joseph is the leader caring for the material needs of Israel, and who provided for them in Egypt: "and Joseph sustained his father and his brethren".[6]

This division between the two leaders is further exemplified in an additional purpose: **Judah was to strengthen the unique national destiny** of being separate from other nations: "Lo, the people shall dwell alone".[7] In contrast, Joseph personifies a contrasting destiny, which will be revealed at the end of days, and that is the **universal purpose of the Jewish people**, "the light unto the nations".[8] These characteristics reveal themselves in their lives and in the future commandments that their tribes must perform.

Joseph, leader of the gentile Egypt, speaks seventy languages, and the Torah is written in seventy languages on an altar on mount Ebal in his

5   Bereshit Rabba 98,2.
6   Genesis 47:12.
7   Numbers 23:9.
8   Isaiah 42:6.

portion in the Land of Israel. In addition, the temple in Shiloh, also in his portion, is characterized by the "laxity" of permitting certain sacrifices to be eaten "in sight" of the Temple.

In contrast, Judah and his tribe are enclosed in fortified Jerusalem, and eat sacrifices only within the walls. There is no intent to embrace gentiles, although gentiles come on their own to Jerusalem to learn the wisdom and the Torah of Israel, as in the days of Solomon[9] or in Messianic times.[10]

The Kingdoms of Israel and Judah

When Solomon's kingdom was divided into two parts because of his sins, as prophesied by Ahijah the Shilonite,[11] Jeroboam the son of Nebat of the tribe of Ephraim (the son of Joseph) received **Ten Tribes** to be the kingdom of Israel, also called the kingdom of "Ephraim". Solomon's son Rehoboam, of the tribe of Judah, received only the two tribes of Judah and Benjamin, to be known as the kingdom of Judah.[12] In this way the dual destiny of the Jewish people became a national reality. It should be noted that in the division of the kingdoms there was an **intermingling of the tribes,** as at the birth of the nation, for purposes of complementarity. The tribe of Benjamin, son of Rachel, was joined with Judah, the son of Leah. Benjamin represents the spiritual orientation within materialism; therefore, part of the Temple is in Benjamin's portion.

In contrast, the tribe of Joseph, represented by his two sons Manasseh and Ephraim, was joined with the tribes of the sons of Leah and the handmaidens, in order to attenuate the materialistic facet. This, however, does not alter the basic purpose of the two kingdoms, as stated above. One is to strengthen the spiritual and unique holiness of the Jewish people, while the other is to strengthen the material body of the Jewish people, with their respective relationships to the other nations, as noted above.

9   Kings I, 5.
10   Isaiah 2 and 11.
11   Kings I, 11.
12   Kings I, 12.

PLACES OF THE EXILE

The Exile of the Two Kingdoms

The Ten Tribes, comprising the kingdom of Israel, were exiled by the Assyrians approximately 135 years before the destruction of the First Temple.

The kingdom of Judah was exiled by the Babylonians after the destruction of the First Temple in 586 B.C.E.

In both cases the exiles were performed in stages. The exile of the Ten Tribes was in two or three stages, possibly more. The same was true of the exile of Judah. It started in the days of Jehoiachin, with the greatest exile in the days of Zedekiah, and ended after the murder of Gedaliah the son of Ahikam.[13]

The sources reveal that there was some intermingling of the tribes in the kingdoms, and it would appear that this was perpetuated also in the exiles.[14] However, the division into tribes was maintained in general. According to the Biblical references and their commentaries, and in reality, the characteristics of the respective exiles were different. **The Judean exile was scattered to the four corners of the earth**, "the scattered of Judah" in the words of Isaiah 11:12. On the other hand, **the**

---

13   See preceding chapter, "Sources".

14   In Jerusalem, there were certainly representatives of the Tribes from all Israel, both important personalities for purposes of the sacrifices and for other reasons. *See Chronicles I, 9.* The *Radbaz* notes: "There must have been representatives of all the tribes in the land of Judah and Benjamin, since men of status dwelt in Jerusalem" (Responsa Or Hahayim, chapt. 88). Therefore it will be necessary to redistribute the tribes at the end of days, as it is written in Malachi 3: "he shall sit as a refiner and purifier". *See Tractate Kidushin 70, 72* and *Maimonides, Hayad Hahazaka Melakhim 12: 3.* In the time of Josiah, about a hundred years after the Exile, some of the Ten Tribes were in Israel and intermingled with the tribe of Judah (since they were a minority) and were subsequently sent into the Babylonian Exile with them. (See Chronicles II, 34:9)

exile of the Ten Tribes remained in populated concentrations in the region in which they were placed, in the general direction of the exile cited in the Bible, northeast of Israel.[15]

It may also be deduced, given the basic characteristics of the two kingdoms as stated above, that since the Judean exile represents the spiritual side of the nation, both their survival as Jews and their redemption depend on to this spirituality. Hence our Sages' statement that "Israel will be redeemed only if they repent" ("Tractate Sanhedrin 92), typifies in particular the tribe of Judah.

The existence of the Ten Tribes, however, is expressed principally by retaining their national identity. Therefore, their redemption is also related to this principle, and they are characterized particularly by the second statement: "Israel will be redeemed only when they become reunited as one".[16]

The Locations of the Exile

According to the sources quoted in preceding chapters, and also when examining sources which refer to the return of the tribes,[17] it seems that the kings of Assyria exiled the Ten Tribes to the **kingdom of Assyria**[18] **and across the Euphrates river.**[19] The prophecy of Ahijah the Shilonite[20] states: "And He will root up Israel out of this good land, which He gave to their fathers, and **will scatter them beyond the river**".[21] The general direction is thought to be north of Israel, although it may easily be east or northeast.

---

15   As indicated by many Sages and even in the Hagiography. See for instance Rabbi Nissim Gaon, Rashi to Sanhedrin 110b, "Tosefet Yom Tov" to the Mishnaic Commentary there, the Gaon of Vilna in "Avnei Eliyahu" etc.

16   Tanchuma, Nitzavim 1.

17   Isaiah 11 and 28.

18   Kings II, 15 and 17.

19   Kings I, 14.

20   Kings I, 14-15.

21   This is interpreted by some as beyond the Euphrates River, and by others as beyond the Sambatyon River.

The exact size and borders of the Assyrian Empire are not known. However, it is reasonable to assume that the exile of the Ten Tribes would have been to some far province belonging to the empire. This is proven by the exile to the **cities of Medes,** which are north of Persia in the region of what is known today as Kurdistan, and also by the conquest of the distant land of Israel and exiling of peoples (the men of Cutah) there.

Other locations expressly mentioned as places of exile were the **Gozan River, Habor, Halah or Lahlah, and Hara.**[22] Where exactly are these places?

According to Saadia Gaon, the Gozan River is the river north of the city of Belah in the north of Afghanistan. The river is known today as the "Amu Darya", and is the border between Afghanistan and the former Soviet Union. One tributary of the river is known even today as the "Rud Jazan" ("Rud" is Persian for "River"). Afghani tradition states that the whole river was once known as the Gozan River.

"Habor" may be the city located in the pass between Afghanistan and Pakistan. This pass is called Pesh-Habor in Afghani (Pesh means pass), after "the city of the pass". The city is known today as Peshawar.

"Hara" may be the city of Harat near the Persian border. It is the third largest city in Afghanistan.

The prophecy of Isaiah states that the exile will bring the tribes to the land of Sinim: "Behold, these shall come from far and lo, these from the north and from the west, and these from the **land of Sinim**".[23] This implies that the exile may have started in the regions of Persia, Kurdistan and Afghanistan, after which the wandering continued eastward toward Pakistan, Kashmir, Tibet, China, etc., and we believe that this also corresponds to the present situation, as will be seen.

22   Kings II, 17 and 18; Chronicles I, 5.
23   Isaiah 49:12. However, there are those who interpret the "Land of Sin" as the Sinai Desert or another region in southern China. The Prophets, who are divinely inspired, also prophesy about *Tsarfat* and *Sefarad* using their modern names not known during Biblical times (*Obadiah*) as well as events during the reign of King Josiah. Indeed, many descendants of the tribes live in China and in the Mongolian countries today (the "land of Sinim"). In the past there were far more. *See below, also, on the Chiang Min tribe.*

It is further implied that their return will be from the east: "From the east I will bring your seed",[24] or from the northeast: "And they will come together from the land of the north, to the Land that I bequeathed to your forefathers".[25]

Tractate Sanhedrin 94 raises the question as to where Sanneherib exiled the Ten Tribes. In response, it brings the replies of Mar Zutra, who said they were exiled to "Afriki", and Rabbi Hanina, who said that they were exiled to the Sloog Mountains. The contrast in the two opinions is surprising. How is it possible that the Bible refers to the northeast, while Mar Zutra talks about the south? The Maharal of Prague notices this discrepancy, and resolves it in his book "Netzach Israel" (chapter 34), by concluding that both **"Afriki"** and **"Sloog Mountains"** are symbolic and not actual locations.

It may be more logical, however, to resolve the discrepancy in the way of modern scholars[26], who say that "Afriki" is actually "Avriki" in the north, in the Caucasian mountains, a place recorded in the conquests of Alexander the Great. It is possible that, although the general direction of the exile was to Assyria and surrounding lands, a small part of the tribes wandered south beyond the Kush mountains, as is the accepted tradition concerning the tribe of Dan.[27]

---

24 Isaiah 43:5.
25 Jeremiah 3:18.
26 Kasdai, who visited Kurdistan and the Caucasus some 70 years ago and clarified various locations cited in the Talmud. Also Rabbi Steinsaltz in his commentary to Tractate Sanhedrin.
27 Eldad Hadani, story 2. "And we have an oral tradition that we are the children of Dan. In the beginning we were tent-dwellers in the land of Israel and there were no warriors in all the tribes of Israel like us. Immediately they said to the children of Dan, rise up and fight against the children of Judah. They said to him on the life of the head of Dan our father, we do not fight with our brothers and we will not shed their blood – finally they advised us to go to Egypt, and not the way that our forefathers went, and also not to destroy it, but in order to cross the Pishon (Nile) river to the land of Kush – **and we came to the land of Kush,** and we found it a good fertile land" (Otzar Midrashim; Y. D. Eisenstein, pp. 22-23).
    In his response to the Jews of Kairouan on the deeds of Eldad Hadani, Mr. Zemah Gaon replied: "In our talks on this we saw legends that can assist our Sages. When

It should be emphasized that **the tribes did not remain in their
original places of exile** (although in Talmudic times they were still
there[28]) but continued eastward and arrived in various places, as is written
in many Biblical verses.[29]

The Sambatyon (The Sabbath River)

The Jerusalem Talmud[30] and many *Midrashim* state that the Ten Tribes
and the Sons of Moses were exiled to "within the Sambatyon" or similar
expressions. The following is one such example: "Rabbi Berechiah and
Rabbi Helbo, in the name of Rabbi Shmuel Bar Nachman: Israel was
dispersed in three exiles. One was past the **Sanbatyon River**, one to the
borders of Antioch, **and one was enveloped by the cloud**". Similarly in
Yalkut Shimoni to Isaiah 49: What is the meaning of "saying to the
prisoners: 'go forth'"? The Ten Tribes were scattered in three exiles: one
was exiled to the **Sambatyon**, and one past the Sambatyon to a distance
equal to the distance from Israel to the Sambatyon, and one to the border
of Rivlata, on Israel's border, and disappeared there. "Saying to the
prisoners: 'go forth'" applies to those at the Sambatyon; "to them that are
in darkness" applies to those past the Sambatyon; and for those in Rivlata,
G-d will make them tunnels which they will enter and follow until they
emerge under the Mount of Olives.

Sanneherib came up and exiled the tribe of Zebulun in the eighth year of the reign
of King Ahaz; from the founding of the Temple until Ahaz's reign there were nearly
264 years. **And since the children of Dan, who were valiant warriors, saw that
the King of Assyria had begun to conquer Israel, they left the Land of Israel for
Kush.** And they camped there..." (ibid. p. 21). This quotation of Mr. Zemah Gaon,
relating to another version of Eldad Hadani, supported this book, but as aforesaid not
all our Sages accept the fidelity of the account.

According to Eldad Hadani, other tribes came to the Land of Kush. From another
Midrash, it seems that the tribe of Shimon (and Judah) arrived in Kush.

Books on the Jews of Ethiopia have been published by Menahem Waldman, as have
articles by the late Rabbi Goren.

28   Yevamot 16.
29   For example, Isaiah 11:1 and 49:12.
30   Sanhedrin 10.

The preceding example teaches us a surprising fact. Instead of specific locations, as quoted in various sources, our Sages talk about unclear locations, even in opposition to the Biblical sources. Some[31] even identify the Sambatyon as the Gozan River, although this fact does not assist our understanding because the Bible gives five different places as their places of exile, but in the above example there are three places, which are very distant from each other, from Eretz Israel to Assyria, and from there another equal distance. All this is not logically comprehensible. It would be helpful to clarify what the Sambatyon is and where it may be located.

First, it should be noted that all the commentators agree that the river **is named for the Sabbath**, hence the name "Sabbatyon", "Sambatyon", and "Sanbatyon" appearing in various Midrashim. This river, as referred to in Tanchuma (Exodus 33) "testifies to the holiness of the Sabbath, that during the weekdays it flows with stones, and rests on the Sabbath" – so that in the dispute between Rabbi Akiva and the wicked Turnus Rufus, Rabbi Akiva uses this fact to prove its holiness.[32] However, to the question of whether Rabbi Akiva could point to the location of the river the answer is "no", because in this dispute (found in Tractate Sanhedrin 65 and other places), the reply to Rabbi Akiva is **"On this matter I do not believe you, because I do not know its location"**. It should be noted that even if Rabbi Akiva could not indicate the location of this river, it did exist in the past. It is actually mentioned by Josephus,[33] Pliny[34] and others.

It appears that **our Sages were not referring to a specific** location when referring to the exile to the Sambatyon. We see this in references to the third exile, about which it is said, "the cloud enveloped them"; or exile to the "borders of Antioch" and "Rivla", which are meant to point to the nature of the exile, rather than to its location. Indeed, when our Sages address themselves to *halakhic* implications of the exile, **they refer to the locations named in the Bible**, and not to the Sambatyon. According to our Sages, therefore, it would be futile to search for an actual physical

31   Nachmanides, for instance, in his commentary to Deuteronomy 32:26.
32   Sanhedrin 65.
33   *Antiquities of the Jews,* Book 7,5.
34   Book 31 ch. 2 of *Natural History.*

location of the Sambatyon. Indeed, the Maharal of Prague writes that our Sages used a **symbolic indication** for the nature of the exile.[35] He writes that the exile to the Sambatyon is an exile to **a very distant, but accessible location**. However, an exile "past the Sambatyon" implies **an inaccessible location**, awaiting the final redemption.

The exile of "the borders of Antioch" or "Rivla" symbolizes an exile of complete assimilation, where only the souls will be saved at the end of days.

It is possible to venture another theory as to why our Sages chose these symbols in reference to the exile of the Ten Tribes.

The initial cause of the exile was the fact that the Ten Tribes had cut themselves off from the holiness of Jerusalem and submerged themselves in materialism. The Sambatyon symbolizes the holiness of the Sabbath, and these tribes are trapped "past the Sambatyon" waiting for the day when all the world will recognize G-d and come to receive His word in Jerusalem. When this happens, they will return to their source of life and to their true holiness, and reunite with Judah, **thereby attaining the veritable fusion of holiness and materialism**. In this context, the reference to "Afriki" or the "Sloog Mountains" are not actual locations of exile, but symbols, like the Sambatyon.[36]

---

35   Netzah Israel, 34.

36   After I had written this chapter, my daughter-in-law told me that she had heard from several Ethiopian immigrants that there was a village in Ethiopia called Sabbathyon, located near a river that in the past would cast up stones during the week and rest on the Sabbath. The person who told this story knew nothing of what the Sages said about Sambatyon.

I spoke with Mr. Shem Tov Zamaro, of Ethiopia, who confirmed this story and recounted that about 10 km east of Gondahar is a village called "Snabat-Gi" (place of the Sabbath): his uncle and aunt lived there, and recounted the meaning of the name: in the past there was a river close to the village that during the week made the noise of a steam train and on the Sabbath was quiet. This is also mentioned in R. Shlomo Horowitz's book "Kol Mevasser", p. 31. On the relation of the Sabbath to the exile of the Ten Tribes, see also Rabbi Avraham Yitzhak Kook, above, in the "Sources" chapter.

Reasons for the Exile of the Ten Tribes

Both the Bible[37] and the Sages[38] state that the exile of the Ten Tribes was caused by materialism and immorality. Samaria is accused of many other sins, but these apparently were not the cause of the exile.

The spiritual state of the kingdom of Israel (Ephraim) was at its lowest ebb – subject to the influence of foreign ideas, such as the worship of the Baal and golden calves and the offering of sacrifices on mountain altars – and at its worst, committing social and immoral sins, especially as stated in Amos. This spiritual condition, which preceded the exile, evokes the terrible warning of Hosea:[39] "Ephraim, he mixes himself among the peoples".

This assimilation is quite understandable, since the Ten Tribes were cut off, without spiritual leadership or books on Jewish Law and values.

---

37   Amos 6.
38   Tractate Sabbath 147.
39   7:8.

LEGACY OF THE EXILE

Life in Exile

As indicated, the spiritual life of the Ten Tribes in Exile was lamen-
table. According to Jeremiah[40] and Ezekiel,[41] the tribes in exile retain a
few **signs and indications** which will serve to identify their past and
return them to the land of Israel. Jeremiah addresses "the virgin of Israel"
(the Ten Tribes) in the following terms: "Set you up way marks, make
yourselves guideposts, set your heart towards the highway, even the way
by which you went; return, O virgin of Israel, return to these your cities".
This also seems to be Ezekiel's intention when he refers to the exile of
the tribes (and also the exile of Jehoyachin): "Although I have removed
them far off among the nations, and although I have scattered them among
the countries, yet have I been to them as a **little sanctuary** in the countries
where they have come".[42]

The Babylonian Talmud, Tractate Yevamot 16, implies that they live as
gentiles ("a gentile who marries") and according to the Amora Shmuel
"Rabbinical courts have made them **as gentiles**". The Jerusalem Talmud
states in the name of Rabbi Eliezer: "If they return, they are to be
considered righteous converts in the days to come".

We understand from this that the Ten Tribes **live in exile as gentiles,
retaining some vestiges of their Jewishness** by which they will be able
to return at the End of Days. However, they will require conversion,
in order to resolve any problem of forbidden marriages.

There are many peoples around the world who are said to present signs
of Jewish descent (the "Ebu" in Nigeria, the "Bassa" in Cameroon, the
"Giyon" in Ethiopia and so forth) although it is very doubtful that said

40   31:20.
41   11:14 ff.
42   Ezekiel 11:16.

signs indicate a Jewish origin. Based on the Biblical citations, however, we are dealing only with peoples northeast of the Land of Israel (excluding the tribe of Dan that went into voluntary exile. The situation of the Tribe of Dan, as explained below, differs from that of the other Tribes.)

Study of the sources shows that the exiled tribes can be classified into three main groups:

1. Tribes which retained their Jewishness – this first group, a minority of the tribes, living **like all other Jews with Torah and commandments** (written and oral Torah), is in the area of the cities of Medes (Kurdistan and the Caucasus).
2. Tribes which kept the written Torah – this **second group**, living **only with the written Torah**, is the Tribe of Dan, in Ethiopia.
3. The Tribes living as gentiles – this **third group**, the great **majority of the tribes, living as gentiles**, with signs of Jewishness, is in the countries of the East.

This classification is understood from the writings of the Maharal of Prague[43] and the Gaon of Vilna[44] and corresponds to today's situation. Following is a discussion of the groups in detail:

The Tribes which Retained their Jewishness

As noted, the Ten Tribes were divided into three groups: the first, exiles who retained their Jewishness, although somewhat loosely; the second, exiles who observed only the written Torah; and the third, exiles who lost their religion, but did not assimilate physically by intermarriage, and kept ancient traditions and various rituals which testify to their Israelite roots.

Although parts of the Ten Tribes did intermingle with the tribes of Judah and Benjamin both before and after the exile, it is clearly shown by the sources and in the writings of the Sages that, during the exile itself, the Ten Tribes **lived separately from other Jews** and will be reunited with Judah at the end of days.

The first group lived a Jewish life of Torah and commandments, albeit with the natural difficulties resulting from life far from Jewish centers.

The Bible mentions the "cities of Medes" as one of the locations of the exile. According to the commentators and accepted explanations, this is the region of Kurdistan and the Caucasus. There is a very widespread tradition among the Jews of Kurdistan that they are from the Assyrian exile. Various scholars also uphold this tradition.[45] Many of this community have returned to Israel and reunited with their fellow Jews.

When considering the possibility that people of this exile wandered north and east, the above criteria apply to **the tribes of Israel living in the Caucasian mountains, between the Caspian and Black Seas;** this includes the Jews of Dagestan, Azerbaijan, Georgia and Armenia, who have a similar tradition, and many of whom have indeed reunited with their brothers in Israel. As a continuation of this exile, large groups wandered eastward beyond the Caspian Sea, where they continued to live as Jews. Thus there are Jews living in Turkmenistan, Uzbekistan and Bukhara who have a tradition that they are from the Ten Tribes.[46] It is possible that the wanderers reached as far as China, Kai-feng in eastern China, and western China near Tibet, where they continued their Jewish way of life.

Because it retained its Judaism and maintained some contact with world Jewry throughout its exile, this group in general even to the present day, is returning to and **becoming fully reunited with** the Jewish people.

Tribes which Kept the Written Torah

While the "Beta Israel" of Ethiopia are indeed descendants of the Ten Tribes, or more precisely the tribe of Dan, their situation is different from that of the other tribes, in that they retained only the written Torah.

---

45   See Encyclopedia Ivrit under Kurdistan, inter alia.
46   Encyclopedia Ivrit – "Uzbekistan".

The assumed genealogical relationship to the **tribe of Dan** is based on travel stories told by Eldad Hadani of the ninth century C.E.; references by great rabbinical luminaries such as Rabbi Akiva of Bartenura in his letters to his father and brothers, the Radbaz,[47] the Mohariksh, and others; and even from Biblical sources.[48]

According to the Gaon of Vilna, the Ten Tribes divided into two types of exiles: all the Ten Tribes living in eastern India, on the other side of the Sambatyon River on one hand, and part of the tribe of Dan on the other side of the "mountains of darkness" (Ethiopia) on the other.[49]

The differences between the first two groups of exiles are expressed in several ways:

1. Freedom from subservience to the gentiles. The Ten Tribes **are free,** but the tribe of Dan is not.
2. The tribe of Dan has only the written Torah and not the oral Law, whereas the Ten Tribes, in the Vilna Gaon's opinion, must undergo conversion.
3. The nature of the exile is expressed symbolically by its location. The Ten Tribes are **past the Sambatyon** (Ganges?) in eastern India. The tribe of Dan is **past the mountains of darkness.**

With the exile of Judah and Benjamin, we then have three exiles: One beyond the mountains of darkness, one beyond the Sambatyon river, and one scattered to the four corners of the earth.

Referring to these three exiles, the prophet Micah says:[50] "I will assemble her that is **lame" (the tribe of Dan with only the written Law);** "I will gather her that is driven away" (the Jews scattered to the four corners of the earth); and **her that I have afflicted" (the Ten Tribes,** beyond the Sambatyon river).

There is also reference in the blessing for the ingathering of the exiles in the "Amida" prayer: "Sound the great horn for our freedom" – for the tribe of Dan which needs to be freed; "lift up the banner to gather our

47   Rabbi David Ben Abi Zimra.
48   Isaiah 11, Zephaniah 3.
49   See footnote 59 below.
50   4:6.

exiles" – for the Ten Tribes; and "gather us in from the four corners of the earth" – for the exile of Judah and Benjamin.

The Tribes living as gentiles

As noted, **most of the Ten Tribes live as gentiles,** with some vestiges of Judaism, and generally reside northeast of the Land of Israel. This is supported by Biblical references, the Talmud, and the great Sages of Israel.

Hence we must search for tribes that have **vestiges of Judaism.** The most important indications are Jewish customs, which are unique, originating neither in other religions nor from contact with Jews. To this may be added archeological finds, Hebrew words in the native tongue, a Jewish "look" (resemblance to known Jews in the area), names of tribes, people and places which are uniquely of the Jewish people or of the Land of Israel, names given to the Creator and similar signs.

There are many groups throughout the world that claim to have such signs. However, the prophets reveal to us that the Ten Tribes live in the east or the northeast.[51] The main part of this book is devoted to these tribes. All the tribes discussed here have some vestiges of Judaism to a greater or lesser extent. It should be emphasized that if they wish to return and live as Jews in Israel it may be only **through conversion,** since proof of their past may be contested. Further, as noted by Rabbi Mordechai Eliyahu, former Chief Rabbi of Israel: **"The greater the proofs and the greater the prospects that they belong to the Ten Tribes, the greater the *mitzvah* in assisting them."**

There follows a general introduction of these tribes, descendants of whom today live as gentiles, which are the main subject of the book.

The Pathans

The Pathans number about 15 million. They live mainly in Afghanistan and Pakistan, but also in Persia, India and neighboring countries.

51   Isaiah 43.

According to their tradition, they are of the Children of Israel and have customs such as circumcision on the eighth day, a fringed garment, knowledge of the Sabbath, and knowledge of pure and impure foods. Some wear amulets containing "Shma Israel" in Hebrew, and they retain names of lost tribes such as Reuven, Naphtali, Gad, Asher and Sons of Joseph. Archeological finds in the region testify to a Hebrew past. The Pathans resemble Jews of the area and, according to many eastern and western scholars, their language (Pashtu) has many Hebrew words.

The Kashmiris

Numbering some 5-7 million, the Kashmiris live in northern India and along its border with Afghanistan. They have a strong Israelite tradition, strengthened by names of various locations in Kashmir resembling names in the Land of Israel, such as Pisgah, Heshbon, Mount Nebo and Beit Peor. This is also true of names of people and of sects. In order to celebrate a holiday called "Baska" in the spring, they adjust the lunar calendar to the solar calendar by adding days to the lunar calendar. Some books have been published on this subject.[52] The people physically resemble Jews and many Hebrew words can be found in the Urdu language of Kashmir. Their history contains the curious fact that in the 12th century only Jews were allowed into Kashmir.

The Shinlung (Bnei Menashe)

The Shinlung tribe numbers 1-2 million and inhabits both sides of the Indian-Burmese border. These areas include Mizoram, Manipur, Nagaland, Asam and Tripura on the Indian side, and the Tidim area in the Chin Mountains on the Burmese side. Their knowledge of the Bible dates prior to the arrival of Judaism and Christianity in the area. They have a tradition of flight from China through Thailand and Burma, and theft of a scroll in their possession. They were called in Burma **Lusi** (which means

---

52   See below, and Encyclopedia Judaica: Kashmir.

"ten tribes"); the name Manasseh, as father of the tribe, appears in their songs and prayers. They wish to return to Judaism and to Israel, and began to observe Jewish laws without outside influence. A small number have immigrated to Israel and converted to Judaism.

The Kareen

The Kareen tribe lives in Burma and numbers some 6-8 million. They have similar traditions to those of the Shinlung, Bible stories before the arrival of Judaism and Christianity, flight from China and loss of their scroll, and the belief in one deity called Yiwa.

The Chiang-Min

The Chiang-Min number approximately 250,000 and live in western China on the Tibetan border, near the Min River in West Szechuan. They are monotheistic and consider the Chinese idol-worshippers. They observe a few Jewish commandments, have a strong tradition of a Jewish origin and offer sacrifices in a manner resembling the ways in which it was done in the Land of Israel during the First Temple period. Few have retained Semitic physical traits.

With Rabbi Tzvi Yehuda Kook, *of blessed memory*, head of the "Merkaz HaRav" Yeshivah, who encouraged the founding of Amishav in 1975

In the company of the Chief Rabbi of Israel, Rabbi A. Shapira *shalita*

Meeting with the heads of the Jewish community in the United States

With the Pathan Ambassador to the U.N. and Doctor Zeller-"Kulanu"

Jonathan Segal and leader of a Pathan village in Pakistan, 1983

Meeting in New York with the leader of the Pathan refugees, 1984

With the oldest Pathan in Kashmir

On a research visit in Kashmir, 1980

Visiting Szechwan while doing research on the Chiang in China, 1998

In Chiang village in Szechwan, China

With Micha Gross and Hallel Halkin (on a trip to China, Thailand and India), 1998

A Karen village in northern Thailand, 1998

Visiting the Karens in Rangoon, Burma, 1994

With Micha Gross and the Karens in Burma

Meeting with members of the Tribe of Menashe, next to a lake in Manipur, 1991

Reception given by the Tribe of Menashe in Vairante in Mizoram, India

Conversion ceremony in Bombay, with members of the court, Rabbi Y. Neuman and A. Shechar, *of blessed memory*, 1988

Sharon Benjamin – sent by Amishav to teach the Benei Menashe in India, 1991

Members of the Ten Tribes Association in Japan

Members of the Ten Tribes Association from Japan visiting "Amishav", 1987

Next to the rabbi who teaches Judaism and a group of American yeshiva boys in Tbilisi, Georgia (Caucasus), 1995

With several Lazginis in Azerbaijan in the Caucasus

First visit to Belmonte, Portugal, 1981

At a wedding after the conversion of the Belmonte community in Portugal

With Mr. Toledano in Majorca, Mr. Soyaz, the driver,
claims he is a descendant of Columbus (?), 1981

With the descendants of the Anusim (Marranos) in Sicily, 1991

Members of the Amishav delegation at the home of Mr. Tomas in Trivandrum, India, 1981

Meeting with the leader of the Kananas in southern India, 1982

Reception in Chalfa, Mexico, by the "Baderech LeYerushalayim" group in Mexico, 1989

"Baderech LeYerushalayim" community in Mexico on their way to the conversion

Benei Moshe community (Peru) at a reception for Amishav, 1989

Benei Moshe after the conversion in the Moche River near Trojilio, Peru, 1989

RETURN AND REDEMPTION

The Return of the Tribes by Jeremiah

The Talmud mentions in a number of places that **Jeremiah returned the Ten Tribes** and that Josiah reigned over them. Tractate Arakhin 32, referring to a Biblical source, indicates: "In the time of Ezra they counted Sabbatical years (shemittah) and jubilee years..." The Talmud then questions this fact, since the population that returned with Ezra numbered 40,660, and the *Halakha* states that jubilees are counted only when the whole nation inhabits the land. The Talmud then replies that Rabbi Jochanan said that **Jeremiah brought the Ten Tribes** and Josiah reigned over them, and therefore jubilees could be counted.

This discussion in the Talmud raises a number of questions:

1. Why is such an important event omitted in both Kings and Chronicles?

2. If these tribes indeed returned and were then exiled with the destruction of the Temple, how do we then interpret the prophecies about the special ingathering of the dispersed of Israel?

3. I Chronicles 5, refers to the Ten Tribes that are in exile thus: "And he exiled Reuben, Gad and half Manasseh, and brought them to Halah, Habor, and the river Gozan even to this day". Tradition says that this part of Chronicles was dictated by Ezra. Furthermore, a similar reference appears in Kings II, 17:23, written by Jeremiah himself.

Notably, both the Radak and Abarbanel do not accept the straight-forward explanation in the Talmud, and both quote other Sages in their explanations for this apparent discrepancy.[53]

The greatest difficulty in explaining the above discrepancy is due to the

---

53 Both discuss the deeds of Josiah in the portion of the Ten Tribes (Kings II 23), and both bring proofs of the presence of remnants of the Ten Tribes.

dispute among the *Tannaites* of the time of the Mishna. The dispute centers on whether the Ten Tribes will be redeemed or not. One opinion is that there cannot be a special return by the Messiah, since they were already returned by Jeremiah, and are therefore together with the other tribes in exile. If Rabbi Akiva considers that they will never return, how would he maintain his opinion in light of their return by Jeremiah? These questions were resolved by Rashi[54] and other luminaries by saying that **Jeremiah returned a small number of the exiles**, but that most indeed will remain in exile until the final redemption.

The return of the tribes by Jeremiah has been interpreted to mean that he tried to return them but did not succeed, or that he returned the remnants of the tribes from Galilee and Samaria to Judah and to the reign of King Josiah. However, these actions would not have enabled the counting of jubilees as stated by Rabbi Jochanan in Tractate Arakhin.

Furthermore, a number of the great Biblical commentators rejected Rabbi Jochanan's explanation, considering it an individual's opinion and not logical in relation to the written sources and the aforesaid problems. Accordingly, we remain with the majority interpretation, which is that **the Ten Tribes remained in their place of exile.**

Will the Ten Tribes return from Exile?

Ultimately, then, will the Ten Tribes return to the land of Israel in the End of Days and reunite with the other Jews of the world?

The need to continue this discussion derives from the basic dispute between **Rabbi Akiva** in the Mishna in Sanhedrin 110, where it is written: the Ten Tribes **will not return**: "And he cast them into another land, as it is this day" (Deuteronomy 29) – As a day ends and does not return, so they have gone and will not return. **Rabbi Eliezer says:** 'As it is this day' – Just as a day darkens and then lights again, so also the Ten Tribes who are in the dark **will have light returned to them** in the future."

The words of Rabbi Akiva are at the center of our discussion. In the

---

54   See Sanhedrin 110b, and Kings II 23:19.

Talmud, our Sages say: "The Ten Tribes will have no part in the world to come, as it is written: 'And the LORD rooted them out of their land in anger, and in wrath, and in great indignation'. 'And the Lord rooted them out of their land' – refers to this world; 'And cast them into another land' – refers to the world to come. This is Rabbi Akiva's interpretation. Rabbi Shimon Ben Yehuda of Akko says in the name of Rabbi Shimon: If their deeds remain as they are this day – they will not return, but otherwise they will return. Rebbi (Rabbi Yehuda) says: They will return in the world to come, as it is written: 'On that day a great horn will sound, and the lost in the land of Assyria will return.'"

The principal question to Rabbi Akiva's interpretation is whether he is referring to the time of the Messiah or to the world to come. Another question is whether he refers to the descendants of the exiled Ten Tribes, or only to the generation that was exiled.

It is also possible to interpret his words in a different way, as will be seen subsequently.

If Rabbi Akiva is referring to the descendants of the Ten Tribes and to the time of the Messiah, then additional questions are raised:

1. How would he interpret all the Biblical sources stating expressly that they will return in the time of the redemption?

2. How would he interpret Ezekiel 47 regarding the distribution of the Land to the tribes at the time of the redemption?

3. Is it possible that Rabbi Akiva meant that the holy structure of the 12 tribes will be lost forever to the Jewish people?

Possible answers to these and other questions, with careful attention to the language of the sources, enable us to apply **four different interpretations** to Rabbi Akiva's statement.

1. Rabbi Akiva is referring to the **sinful first generation,** and meant that they will not have a part in the world to come.

2. He may be referring only to those **who did not return in the time of Jeremiah**.

3. He is referring only to **those of the Ten Tribes who assimilated with the gentiles.**

4. His statement applied only to the return of the Tribes **in the time of the Second Temple.**

Some interpret Rabbi Akiva's statement to mean, quite simply, that the Ten Tribes will not be redeemed at the time of the Messiah. Rashi, for instance, in his commentary in Tractate Sanhedrin 110, says that the Messiah will not accept them with the other exiles because **they defamed the Land of Israel.** This refers to exiles of the Ten Tribes who found the Land lacking in comparison to their place of exile, and praised their places as "twice as good as the Land of Israel".[55] This sin, comparable to the sin of the spies who were sent during the Exodus, disqualified the Ten Tribes and their descendants from returning to the Land. However, this raises a difficulty, since the sons are not to be punished for the sins of the fathers forever. In any case, if we accept Rabbi Akiva's interpretation that they will not return at the time of the Messiah, it must be asked **whether halakhic ruling is indeed according to Rabbi Akiva in this case.**

In his commentary on Sanhedrin, Maimonides states that since this is not a *halakhic* matter, it need not be resolved: "I have mentioned many times that any dispute between the Sages which has no practical application, but is a matter of belief or faith, need not be resolved halakhically according to one or another". Nevertheless, Torah luminaries from the Talmudic Sages to the present have disputed this very matter of whether *halakha* has to be decided in matters of faith, and the inclination has been to apply decisions in matters of faith.

This very subject of the Ten Tribes may no longer be a question of faith, because we now face the **practical** problem of whether we should search for the Ten Tribes and assist them in returning to the Land. Because many of the *Tanaaites* of the Talmud disagree with Rabbi Akiva in this matter, *Halakha* is not applied according to him. The great Radbaz writes on the subject: "Even if Rabbi Akiva indeed made this statement, nevertheless the two *Tannaites*, Rabbi Eliezer and Rabbi Shimon Ben Yehuda of Akko, disagree with him. **Therefore I believe that they will return** and have a part in the world to come."

---

55   Sanhedrin 94.

According to the Gaon of Vilna, the prayer of "Sound the great horn" was formulated expressly for the Ten Tribes by the Sages of the Great Council, because the redemption of all of Israel depends on them. Therefore the disciples of the Gaon of Vilna sent messengers to search for the Ten Tribes.

How the Tribes will Return

Many Biblical prophets talk about the redemption of the tribes by either G-d himself, or by the Messiah.[56] This is not to say that we may not involve ourselves. It is an accepted tradition that in matters of redemption, heavenly intervention will be the result of human initiation – a worldly initiation that will initiate heavenly activity.

Therefore, **the main redemption of the Ten Tribes will be by the Messiah of the House of David,** but we must also act to the best of our ability. There is no problem regarding Jews who observe the commandments; they will return to the Land of their own accord.

Since the "Beta Israel" of Ethiopia "were without freedom", and require ritual conversion (immersion only, according to the ruling of the Chief Rabbinate), **they require the help of the tribe of Judah**; they are indeed coming back to the Land, and a large number of the tribe is already among us.

Regarding the Ten Tribes who live as gentiles, because they are hidden (past the Sambatyon) and are separated from us by their gentile way of life and acceptance of other faiths, we are commanded to search for them (as the brothers of Joseph searched for him), and return them to the Land. Midrash Yalkut Shimoni 985 on the Song of Songs states: "Also our couch is leafy" – these are the Ten Tribes who were exiled past the Sambatyon, and whom the exiled of Judah and Benjamin **will seek out and return,** "so that they may share the days of the Messiah and life in the world to come". Jeremiah 3 states: "In those days the house of Judah shall walk with the house of Israel, and they shall come together out of

---

56   Isaiah 11, 43, 49; Jeremiah 30; Ezekiel 11, 37, Micah 4; Zechariah 8 etc.

the land of the north to the land that I have given for an inheritance unto your fathers".

Since they are the important part, it may be said that **the redemption of all the Jews of the world depends on them**. According to the Abarbanel, the Gaon of Vilna, the Malbim, and others, **the redemption of the Ten Tribes precedes the redemption of the rest of Israel**, as the Gaon of Vilna writes[57]: "When our Messiah comes, first will come the Ten Tribes, and then Judah and Benjamin, as it is written in Isaiah 27: 'And they shall come that were lost in the land of Assyria – first who are the Ten Tribes, and after that: And they that were dispersed in the land of Egypt – they who are the remnants of the house of Judah and Benjamin'".

From this we deduce that we, who came to Zion before the Ten Tribes, are meant to do that which was stated above: **"to seek out and return them to the Land"**, and this was indeed what the disciples of the Gaon of Vilna attempted to do.

In light of the above, we of Judah and Benjamin are commanded to go and fetch the Ten Tribes "so that they may share the days of the Messiah and life in the world to come".

Although this applies to all the Ten Tribes, our main task applies to those of the tribes who are living as gentiles, and who require our assistance, because they cannot return **without proper conversion**, even if they wanted to.

The *halakhic* background of this matter should be clarified. The accepted *halakhic* position is that candidates for conversion should be turned away, until we are convinced that their desire to convert is sincere, at which time they are accepted with open arms. The reason for this is stated in the Talmud:[58] "Converts are as an affliction to Israel".

This attitude is understandable in light of Jewish thought: A gentile who joins the Jewish people is likened to dead meat in the body of the nation, unless his soul was present in Sinai, which means that he has a Jewish soul, and then his union with the nation is not as a foreign body. Since

---

57 "Avnei Eliyahu" to "sound the great horn", Gaon of Vilna prayer book.
58 Yevamoth 47.

we have no method of examining souls, we reject a gentile who desires
to convert, until it is proven that his desire is sincere, and this proves that
his soul has a Jewish origin.

In any case, all agree that we are commanded to seek out and return to
the fold anyone who has a Jewish soul and is of Israelite origin. Indeed,
spiritual salvation is even more important than the physical saving of lives,
and the greater the proofs and signs of Israelite origin, the greater the
mitzvah in assisting them in return to Judaism.

Since our Sages declared that the Ten Tribes will be "righteous converts
in the days to come",[59] they have Jewish souls, and we must seek them
out and return them to the fold. There is no need to be concerned about
marital difficulties, because the Talmud declares them as gentiles in
Yevamoth 16.

Moreover, even if there are doubts about some of the tribes who exhibit
Jewish customs and signs, we must nevertheless try to return them, as
halakha dictates about one whose Jewishness is in doubt.

This process of returning the tribes must be done after careful exam-
ination of facts and individuals, and proper preparation for conversion,
after which the true converts should be allowed to join our people.

---

59   Jerusalem Talmud, Sanhedrin 10.

THE BANISHED TRIBES
OF ISRAEL

The Pathans in Afghanistan and Pakistan
The Kashmiri nation in Northern India
The Karen People in Myanmar (Burma)
The Shinlung (Menashe) in Northeast India
The Chiang-min Tribe in China
The Ten Tribes in Japan
The Ten Tribes in Kurdistan and the Caucasus
Beta Israel of Ethiopia

THE PATHANS IN AFGHANISTAN AND PAKISTAN

The Pathans are also called simply Afghans, or Sons of the Pashtu (after their language). They also identify themselves by their ancient name "Sons of Israel" (Bnei Israel), although they live today as Muslims.

The Pathans number 8-9 million in Afghanistan and 10-11 million in Pakistan. They live in the border region between the two countries, and about two million live as nomads. In external appearance they resemble the Jews of the region. Their ancient customs and other data indicate a definite connection with the Jewish people.

The purpose of this chapter is to present the reader with evidence of the connection of the Pathans to the Tribes of Israel.

1. The Life of the Pathans

The Pathans generally live between the city of Kabul in Afghanistan and the Indus River in Pakistan. The Pathans have settled throughout over half the country of Afghanistan, and generally hold power in the areas where they live.

A large part of this people lives near the eastern border of the country, in an area named Pushtunistan, on the Pakistani border. Afghanistan supports the Pakistani Pathans' desire for independence, and this leads to constant tension in the region.

Afghanistan is considered one of the least developed countries in Asia. The vast majority of the population is illiterate. The inhabitants work primarily in farming or raising sheep and other domesticated animals. Despite the efforts of the regime to urbanize the inhabitants, most still live in villages, and some as nomads. Until recently, Afghanistan was one of the few countries in the world to be governed by Islamic religious law. More than 90% of the population is Sunni Muslim.

The little modernization that has entered the country has not influenced the mountainous border areas, where the Pathans continue their centuries-old tribal life. The leader is the tribal chief, and in the family unit all obey the family elder. The legal system is known as the "Pashtunwali" – the law of the Pashtun, similar in parts to the Torah, as will be shown subsequently. The Pathans are in general very healthy, tall and strong, with light skin and a pleasant mien. They are warriors, and most carry arms from a young age. They are hard working, wise, truthful and extremely loyal. They also have a worldwide reputation for exemplary hospitality.

2. The ethnic origin of the Pathans

The ethnic origin of the Pathans has long puzzled scholars, because the Pathans differ both in appearance and character from the ethnic groups of this region: the Indo-Aryans, the Turks, the Mongolians, and the Persians. It is also difficult to trace their history in a region in which scores of nations and major tribes of various origins have come and gone.

Scholars have advanced various hypotheses regarding the origin of the Pathans.[1] Many Eastern and Western scholars accept the Pathan tradition of Israelite origin.[2] Some conclude that the Pathans are descendants of the Ten Tribes of Israel, exiled by the Assyrian Empire about 140 years before the destruction of the First Temple in 586 B.C.E. Researchers point out as most significant the tradition of their ancient name "the Sons of Israel" and their appearance, which is similar to Jews of the region. Some refer to ancient customs retained by the Pathan tribes as proof of their Israelite ancestry.

1   The origins claimed are Turkish or Mongolian in: S.M. Imamuddin, *The Origin of Afghans, Islamic Culture*, vol. 23, pp. 1; India-Aryan in: Caroe, *The Pathans*; Armenian-Caucasian with various mixtures (this can also fit the view of an Israelite origin) in: *Encyclopedia of Islam*, "Afghan", pp. 216.
2   *Inter alia* in S.M. Imamuddin, ibid.; Bellew, *The Races of Afghanistan*, pp. 23 (1949); Noldich, *Afghan Claim*; Nemunn, *Afghanistan – From Darius to Amanula*; Pennel, "The Tribes on our N.W.F"., Asian Review 1910, vol. 30, pp. 88.

Following the arrival of Jews from Afghanistan to the State of Israel, many important testimonies have been recorded (some reproduced below) that support theories regarding Pathan customs and shed new light on heretofore disregarded data. All this serves to strengthen the likelihood of the Pathans' Israelite origin.

3. Relationship to Tribes of Israel

The personal identification of the Pathan tribes with their Israelite origin is expressed in various ways. In addition to the oral tradition related by the elders of the tribe, there are interesting testimonies to the keeping of genealogy scrolls which record back to the fathers of the Jewish nation. These scrolls have been well preserved, and some are written in gold on doeskin.

No less interesting and significant are the names of the tribes, which closely resemble those of the Tribes of Israel: the Rabbani tribe (in Afghan dialect) may be the Tribe of Reuben, the Shinwari – Shimon, the Lewani – Levi, Daftani – Naftali, Jaji – Gad, Ashuri – Asher, Yusuf-Zai – Sons of Yosef, Afridi – Ephraim, and so forth.[3] Some Afghani Jews believe the other Tribes of Israel are also to be found among the Pathans. Furthermore, testimonies note that the Pathans themselves claim that the small differences between the original name of the tribe and its present name result from the different dialects of the languages; so that Jaji, for example, was originally Gad.

A well-known tradition of the Afghan royal family traces the family's origin to the tribe of Benjamin and the family of King Saul. The tradition was first published in the book "Makhzan-I-Afgani" (c. 1635) and has since been cited by most of the research literature.[4] According to the tradition, King Saul had a son named Irmia (Jeremiah) who had a son named Afghana. Irmia died around the time of King Saul's death and

---

3   See below.
4   Written by Nematullah Harvi, a scribe at the court of Mughal Emperor Jehangir of Hindustan.

Afghana, reared by King David, remained in the royal court during King Solomon's reign. About 400 years later, during the Babylonian exile, the descendants of Afghana fled to the region of "Gur" (Hazarat Jat, today) in what is now central Afghanistan. The tribe settled and traded with the people around it. In the year 662, Mohammed sent Khalid Ibn al-Walid, the head of the Kuraiysh tribe, to spread Islam among the Afghan tribes. He met the "Sons of Israel" in Gur and converted them to Islam, returning to the Prophet with seven representatives of the Afghans and 76 of their supporters. The leader of the "Sons of Israel" was "Kays" or "Kish" (named after Saul's father). According to the tradition, the emissaries were rewarded by Mohammed. Kish changed his name to Ibn Rashid and was entrusted by Mohammed with the task of spreading Islam among his people.

4. The Location of the Assyrian exile

According to the Bible, the Ten Tribes were exiled to "Halah", to "Habor", to "the River Gozan", to "Hara" and to the "cities of the Medes".[5] Scholars differ regarding the location of these places.

A Jewish Afghani tradition identifies the Gozan River as "Rud Jazan" ('Rud' means 'river' in Persian), a source of the Amu Darya, which passes by the city of Maimana. It is possible that the entire Amu Darya was once called Rud Jazan. The city "Habor" is traditionally identified as Peshawar, whose name consists of the two words Pesh-Hibur, also known as the Khyber Pass (in Afghani). Today Peshawar is the Pathan center on the Pakistani border.

The city of "Hara" is the city Herat, the largest in western Afghanistan.

Probably the entire area was populated by the ancient Assyrian exile. As noted elsewhere, some scholars claim that all the Jews living today in the southern part of the former Soviet Union, along the Amu Darya, are descendants of the Ten Tribes (for instance, the Bukharans and the

---

5   Kings II, 18; Chronicles I, 5.

Georgians) who lost contact with the other Tribes of Israel and forgot their tribal origin. There are known to be groups called "Sons of Israel" both in India and Afghanistan, and some have come to Israel. The Afghan tribes are located in the very heart of the region in which the Ten Tribes settled. It is conceivable that the Assyrian exile dispersed the tribes directly to these places, or perhaps they arrived in this region at a later stage, possibly during the Babylonian exile, as maintained by popular tradition.

5. Physical similarities of Pathans and Jews

The Pathans bear a marked physical similarity to Jews. Even the British, who ruled Afghanistan for a long period of time, had difficulty distinguishing between them and called the Pathans "Jews".

When not wearing their traditional garb, Pathans are practically indistinguishable from other Jews of the area. Of the some twenty-one peoples of Afghanistan, only the Pathans (like the Jews) have Semitic features. They have a paler complexion than other Afghani groups, long noses, and some have blue eyes. Most Pathans also grow beards and sidelocks similar to those of the Jews in the region, making it further difficult to differentiate between the two.

6. Jewish Customs

Despite the fact that Pathans are Islamic converts, they have retained some of their ancient Jewish customs, documented by testimonies of Afghan Jews (reproduced below).

Some customs have been identified as Jewish even by non-Jewish scholars.[6] It should be emphasized that, in the past, most of the scholars who investigated these matters had little knowledge of Jewish customs, limiting progress in this important field. The testimonies were received mostly from Afghani and Pakistani Jews who lived in the Pathan regions

6   S.M. Imamuddin, ibid.; A. S. Fletcher: The Way of Conquest.

and came into contact with Pathan people. They do not refer to all Pathans, all Pathan tribes, or even to all localities; nonetheless, they do prove the existence of Jewish customs among Pathans. This study requires additional quantitative and qualitative investigation in order to be conclusive.

Some examples of Jewish customs are presented below:

Tribal Names – some of the Pathan tribes in Afhanistan call themselves by names similar to the names of the Twelve Tribes.

Pathan law – The Pathan law is well-known in the region and is called in their language "Pushtun-wali". Pushtun-wali includes laws similar to Torah laws, such as 'an eye for an eye' (in the literal sense rather than the sense of the Oral Law), cities of refuge and blood vengeance. Without a doubt, some Pushtun-wali laws have no other origin than the Torah.

Sidelocks – Photographs and testimonies show that Pathans grow sidelocks. Most Pathans also have beards. Pathans believe this ancient custom is a sign of their Jewish ancestry.

Circumcision on the eighth day – There are testimonies to the existence of a very joyous circumcision ceremony on the eight day after birth. This is a known Jewish custom, and is not a Muslim tradition.

***Tallit* and four-cornered garments (*tzitzit*)** – Many testimonies indicate the regular wearing of a *tallit*, called by the Pathans "Joy-Namaz" ("place of prayer" in Afghani). This rectangular garment (about 3 meters long) is made to cover the head and part of the shoulders, and is spread on the ground for prayer in the Muslim fashion. It has no fringes.

The Afghanis also wear a sort of small *tallit* called "kafan". This is a four-cornered garment with strings similar to the *tzitzit*. **Pathans themselves regard this as a sign of their Jewish origin.**

Jewish wedding – Some testimonies record the Pathan custom of using a wedding canopy (*huppa*) and rings, similar to the Jewish custom.

Behavior of a menstruating woman – The women observe laws similar to the Jewish laws regarding menstruation. During and for one week following menstruation, no contact is allowed between the wife and husband. After this period, the woman immerses herself in a river or spring, or goes to a bath house if a natural water source is not available.

Levirate marriages – This ancient Jewish custom dictates that when a man dies without children, his brother marries the widow. The custom is no longer practiced by Jews, but is found among the Pathans, and is seen by gentiles as proof of Jewish origin.

Honoring parents – The commandment of honoring one's father is kept in an exemplary manner by the Pathan tribes. A son must obey his father in all matters. When the father enters the room, all stand and bow their heads in his honor.

Forbidden foods – Pathans do not eat horse or camel meat (foods forbidden by Judaism). There is some evidence that they do not eat meat and dairy foods that were cooked together. They also have a tradition regarding the differentiation between pure and impure birds.

Sabbath day – The Sabbath is considered a day of rest, and there are testimonies of abstention from labor, cooking and baking. They prepare 12 loaves in honor of the Sabbath, a custom performed in the ancient Temple. Some Pathans institute legal proceedings on the Sabbath.

Lighting a candle to honor the Sabbath – A significant indication of the Jewish origin of the Pathan tribes is lighting a candle to honor the Sabbath. After lighting, the candle is covered, usually by a large basket. The candle is lit by a woman after menopause.

Day of Atonement – One testimony relates that a man of the Pathan Lewani tribe came to the Jewish synagogue on the Day of Atonement every year and stayed there until sundown, without uttering a word. Afterwards the man spoke of the tradition of the Temple and of the High Priest and his work there on the Day of Atonement. One year the man erred in the date and did not come to the synagogue; he wept bitterly when he realized his mistake.

Prayer – In general, the Pathans, like other Muslims, pray in mosques facing Mecca. Some Pathans, however, pray facing Jerusalem. There are some very old synagogues, relics testifying to an ancient past, near Andkhoi, Mulmul, and in Peshawar. Some Pathans visit these synagogues on special days, during times of great distress or tragedy or to offer special prayers. The individual who seeks help comes there to touch the lock and pray. Some say that these synagogues once contained Torah scrolls.

Blood on the door lintel and posts – At a time of plague, Pathans slaughter a sheep and sprinkle its blood on the lintel and doorposts. The Bible records a strikingly similar action performed by the Israelites with the blood of the Passover sacrifice, during the Plague of the First-born in Egypt.

Scapegoat – A custom similar to the Biblical sending out of a scapegoat to atone for sins is found among the Pathans.

Hebrew amulet – There are a few testimonies to the use of amulets written in Hebrew script and containing the phrase "Hear O Israel." The amulet is written in secret by the head of the tribe, and it is forbidden to open it.

Hebrew names – Among the Pathans there are Hebrew names, such as Israel and Samuel. These names are not found among Muslims.

Place names – Some testimonies claim that Afghanistan has locations, neighborhoods and villages with names based on places in the Land of Israel.

Holy books – There are testimonies to the existence of pages and even complete holy books among the Pathans. They honor greatly "Taurat El Sharif" (the Torah of Moses) and rise at the mention of Moses' name.

Cities of Refuge – In Israel during Biblical times, six cities were designated 'cities of refuge' to which could flee an unintentional murderer (someone who caused the death of a person by accident, Numbers 35:11-12). There is only one source for this practice – the Bible – and just one explanation for its observance among Pathans: a connection to ancient Israelites. In Israel, Jews did not keep this practice after the destruction of the Second Temple. To day, the practice is found neither among Jews nor any other people.

Animal Sacrifice – during Biblical times, only the Ten Tribes in the northern Kingdom of Israel continued to practice animal sacrifice separate from the Temple in Jerusalem. The Pathans practice animal sacrifice.

Jubilee Year – this custom was observed during Biblical times, only in the Land of Israel. Every 50 years, property was restored to its original owner (Leviticus 25:10). The Pathans re-allocate property every 10 years to its original owner.

Star of David – This symbol is found in almost every Pathan house in the Peshawar area. The wealthy make it from expensive metals, the poor from simple wood. It can be seen on towers, schools, tools and jewelry.

7. Archeological and other evidence

In addition to ancient synagogues, Torah scrolls, Hebrew place names, and tribal genealogy books as indicated above, there are also testimonies that refer to significant archeological finds:

- Near Herat in Chaghcharan, ancient graves were found with engravings in Hebrew and Persian script. The graves date from the eleventh to thirteenth centuries.
- A number of writings etched on rocks were found near the city of Netchaset. These seem to be in ancient Hebrew script and another, unidentified, language.
- In the Dar-El-Amman Museum in the capital city of Kabul there is a black stone, discovered in Kandahar and bearing the following inscription in Hebrew: "Ana went in G-d's shadow; Betzalel went in G-d's shadow; fear and trembling will come upon us; he who is a Jew will die, and he who is a Muslim will live. On Wednesday, 13th of Adar..." The year is broken off, perhaps intentionally.

- Also in the Museum is a stone written in ancient Hebrew script, which indicates a Jewish past and the presence of Jews for at least 1,500 years.
- In Minerjam, in the center of Afghanistan, there is a large Star of David etched in stone. In Tchastovi, there is a school with a Star of David on it.

8. Amishav and the Pathans

Since its founding, Amishav has placed primary importance on research of the Pathans and attempts to make contact with them, with the understanding that the subject must be handled with the utmost discretion because of the nature, size and location of the tribe.

In 1975, the year Amishav was founded, the organization sponsored Moshe Haredim, a Technion University student of Iranian descent, to travel to Afghanistan. He traveled throughout the country for one month with the objective of gathering information about the status of the Pathans and their traditional and current perspectives regarding the Jewish people. He visited and photographed Pathans in their own territory and investigated the museum in Kabul. As a preliminary fact-finding mission Mr. Haredim's trip was successful, despite limitations caused by the difficult and dangerous conditions.

In 1983, Amishav sponsored emissary Yonatan Segal and photographer Moshe Ken on an additional fact-finding mission. The gentlemen succeeded in obtaining excellent photographs of Pathans; however, their success in gathering information was thwarted by the harsh weather conditions.

Over the years, the author has made contact with Pathan exiles in the United States. There has been little success in reaching the vast numbers of Pathans in Afghanistan.

The most important contact followed the publication of an English translation of the author's book "The Lost in Assyria". A copy of the book was obtained by Mr. Rushan Khan, a Pathan from Mardhan in northern Pakistan. Mr. Khan wrote two books supporting the Israelite origin of the Pathans and his correspondence with Amishav continued for some eight years. Unfortunately, he passed away before he could undertake a translation of Amishav's material into the Pathan language.

Shortly after, contact was made with the then Ambassador of Afghanistan to the United Nations, himself of Pathan origin, who received a copy of the author's book "The Lost in Assyria" and developed great enthusiasm for the subject. The ambassador requested permission to translate the Pathan sections of the author's book into the Pathan language, with the hope of restoring the tribe's connection to the Jewish people. As a result of the ambassador's noble efforts, the Pathan chapter of the author's book was eventually translated and published in Dhari, the language used by the Pathans in Afghanistan.

During the author's 1993 lecture tour in the United States, he met with the same ambassador, as well as the Secretary of the Embassy of Afghanistan, in Washington D.C. Both meetings were conducted in an atmosphere of genuine warmth and friendship. The Secretary, also of Pathan origin, was very knowledgeable of the Pathan traditions and teachings regarding their Israelite origin. He related his personal experience, including lessons from his own grandfather, and offered to assist the author in any way possible.

The most significant event in developing contact with Pathans was the author's meetings with a group of Pathan exiles in the United States associated with the Pashtun section of Voice of America Radio. The author met with radio and academic personalities involved with the section. The station broadcast in Afghanistan an interview with the author which included his presentation of the connection between the Pathans and the People of Israel.

The author continues to research the Pathans and explore possibilities of making contact with members of the Pathan tribes in Afghanistan and Pakistan.

Eyewitness accounts of the Pathans

Introduction

Afghani immigrants in Israel tell of what they saw with their own eyes or heard from others, about the Afghan tribes and the traces of Judaism in their culture. These testimonies were collected and recorded by Mr. Yitzhak Ben Zvi (former President of Israel) in his book *Nidhei Israel* and some are quoted here. Testimonies are also quoted from Mr. Avraham Zonenshein's book, *Or Hadash be-Zion* (New Light in Zion). Additional testimonies are brought from other sources and some have been collected and recorded more recently.

Because the testimonies are very important to the research of the Afghan tribes, we endeavor to quote them as precisely as possible. Distinction is made between testimonies that were written and collected in a specific place and testimonies that were collected by another source. Witnesses may have seen or heard the same things at different times or places, and related their impressions to more than one researcher at different times. This is why there may be variations and even contradictions in the relating of events in different testimonies. Nevertheless, the testimonies of the immigrants from Afghanistan serve to illustrate and substantiate the Jewish origin of the tribes of Afghanistan.

Excerpts from "The Dispersed of Israel" (Hebrew) by the late President Yitzhak Ben-Zvi

The tribes of Afghanistan, among whom the Jews of Afghanistan dwelt for many generations, are Sunni Muslims who still maintain the amazing tradition regarding their origin from the Ten (lost) Tribes. This tradition, which is well-known among the Afghan people, is an ancient one with historical corroboration. Both Jewish and non-Jewish researchers and travelers have testified to the existence of this tradition, as do scholars of the people and country of Afghanistan who take their data from literary sources only. Little has been published on this matter in books and encyclopedias in the European languages and Hebrew.

Jewish travelers of the Middle Ages and Land of Israel emissaries, who have visited these eastern cities, refer to the Israelite origin of the tribes of Afghanistan.[7] The remarks of European scholars and travelers who visited these tribes, cited in all the important encyclopedias, support this claim. It also appears in old Afghan chronicles, quoted by modern Afghani authors. Modern researchers and travelers, however, do not relate to the Israelite origin of the Afgani tribes, possibly because the numerous imaginary legends on the matter in certain literature led to skepticism among the people of an "enlightened" generation. The main reason may be the very remoteness of Afghanistan to modern Western visitors. It is separated by mountains and deserts from the Jews of Europe, and researchers have almost no means to contact the small Jewish community in the remote parts of these "mountains of darkness". It is not surprising that the matter of the Afghan tribes' tradition of Jewish origin has not been accorded priority by Jewish scholars.

However, with the establishment of the State of Israel in 1948 and the immigration to Israel of the Jews of Afghanistan, it became possible to collect testimonies from eyewitnesses who had spent many years among these tribes and learned of their traditions and customs "first-hand". These testimonies are from Jews who relate what they saw with their own eyes and heard with their own ears, even without realizing the significance of their testimony.[8]

1) Testimony of Mr. Yaakov Danieli of Tel Aviv

One of the Muslim tribes in Pakistan has the tradition of being from the tribe of Benjamin. Their ancient forefathers, however, never entered the

---

7   See Y. Yaari: *Shlihim me-Eretz Israel Le-Aseret Hashevatim* (Emissaries from the Land of Israel to the Ten Tribes), Sinai-year 3:2-13.

8   *Nidhei Israel* [The Banished of Israel], Part II, pp. 146-147.

land of Israel. They tell of a civil war in the desert between the tribes of Israel, during which most of the tribe of Benjamin was killed and the rest fled into the desert, never to return. They wandered through lands, nations and kingdoms, until their early ancestors reached the part of India, which is the present-day Pakistan and settled there, later to become the forbearers of these tribes.

Avraham Zonenshein indicates the connection of this tradition with the Biblical portion of "Ekev" (Deuteronomy 10:6), where Rashi recounts a legend of a war that broke out among the tribes of Israel over a decision to return to Egypt after Aaron's death, when the Pillar of Cloud disappeared. The Levites chased after the dissenting tribes, and after the battle returned them to the path of the journey to the Land of Israel. This legend seems to substantiate the Afghan tradition.

2) Testimony of Mr. Hananya Davidov

I was part of a group of cooperative traders who peddled all sorts of products to the villages, and in the course of our work we reached the most distant regions of the country. It should be noted that most of the commerce in the areas near the Indian border is conducted by Indian traders. These isolated, remote and mountainous areas of the Pakistani border were difficult to reach, and the situation was exploited by the Indian traders, who demanded very high prices. They had a total monopoly on these areas and objected to our invading their territory.

During one of our trading trips, I arrived with my group of ten traders in one of the villages in the remote mountainous region near the Pakistan border. We naturally came into contact with the sheikh (the religious leader of the village) and we told him we were Jews. This fact awakened great curiosity in him and in the people of the community, and the sheikh came often to visit us. Each time he asked us many questions about Judaism. He told us that he and the people of his community and the villages of the area were of the tribe of Benjamin – of the Sons of Israel, and that at the time of the Islamic conquests they had been forcibly converted to Islam.

Our group stayed in the village a few days, during which time we saw that they light a candle on the eve of the Sabbath, which they then cover. They were interested in every detail of our conduct, and especially in our religion and how we observe it. In most cases they questioned us, because we were afraid to question them and examine their customs. Afghanistan is clearly and fanatically a Muslim country and we were afraid that our contact with our distant brethren would result in heavy jail sentences. For minor infractions you can rot for years in jail and suffer hair-raising tortures. Were it not for this fear, we would have been able to examine their customs and question them about their past and collect much factual material as to their Jewish origin. We also knew that on the other side of the Pakistani border there are large areas inhabited only by members of these tribes.

For their livelihood, the people of this area have orchards and almond trees, and we heard that they sometimes attack caravans passing on the roads. As already noted, the Indians who controlled the commerce in the area objected to our trading on their territory, and did everything possible to get us out of the area. After a few days, we received orders from the Afghan authorities to leave before we harmed the economy of the local traders, who were established residents and local citizens.

3) Testimony of Mr. N. Mashiah

I am from Persia. I have lived in Israel for decades, but I cannot forget what happened to me once on a business trip to Afghanistan. While in Afghanistan, I arrived in a small town near the Pakistani border. At that time the British still ruled India, and their influence was felt in the village and in the region. The area is very mountainous and the inhabitants of the mountain villages are brave and aggressive fighters. In order to protect the regular traffic on the mountain roads, the British learned from the bitter experience of battles with the tribesmen that it was advisable to come to terms with the sheikhs, the heads of the tribes, rather than entering into conflict with them. It had already cost them many casualties, and so they paid large bribes to the heads of the tribes. While I was staying in the village, the British withheld payment from the tribal head of the region.

One day I sensed a strange silence in the town, like the quiet before the storm. All at once, hordes of riders came out of the hills, and flooded the town. They were fierce-looking fighters, and they so frightened the representatives of the Afghan authorities and the local police that they fled in every direction. Within a short time the riders had stripped the stores and homes bare. They gathered their booty as one gathers sea-fish in a pool without any opposition. While collecting the booty they saw me and realized immediately that I was a stranger and a non-Muslim. They did not harm me, but began to question me. I told them that I was a Jewish trader from Persia, and they let me speak to their leader, the tribal sheikh.

This is what the sheikh told me:

'We know about our Jewish origin. It was passed on by word of mouth that we are from the Sons of Israel and were complete Jews until the time of the Islamic conquests when we were forcibly converted to Islam. We have a tradition that about 100 years before the coming of Muslim emissaries to our region, idol-worshipping people who were also fire-worshippers attacked our people, and robbed and plundered them of all, including their ancient books. As a result, our people forgot many of the principles of the religion, because they were left only with an oral tradition'.

Difficult conditions and constant fear of discovery further lessened their contact with Torah and their traditions. When the representatives of Islam came and threatened them, and hearing that Muslims believed in one G-d, they accepted Islam in order to save themselves but secretly continued to keep the tradition of their Jewish origin.

4) Testimony of Mr. Michael Gul of Tel Aviv

When I was a child, a rumor reached our city of Herat in Afghanistan that the king, the Amir Habibullah Khan, father of the king Amman Alla Khan, would come to visit our city on horseback. The important Jews of the city met and decided on a ceremonial reception for the king. Among them was my father and teacher of blessed memory, who was a respected merchant in the region, and who urged me to attend the reception.

The king asked the Jews: 'from what tribe are you?' The heads of the Jewish delegation answered: 'we have no family genealogy and we do not know, our lord and king.' To this the king answered: 'we do know. We are of the Mohammed Zai family, all of us of the Benjamin tribe, of the seed of King Saul, from the sons of Jonathan, Afghan and Pathan.'

The king thanked the Jews for their reception and commanded to dress each of them (there were 12) in gold coats and golden turbans, and he sent them with an honor guard of his soldiers so that the gentiles would see and respect the Jews.

The name Pithon, the grandson of Jonathan, the son of Saul, is mentioned in Chronicles I (8:35). According to the tradition of the locality, which is between Peshawar in Pakistan and Jalalabad, the Pathans there are descendants of Pithon, and they even have some Jewish customs. They sew something that looked like a four-sided garment on their clothes, two corners in front and two at the back like a *tallit*, and it had two white strings in each of the corners. They also grow sidelocks, and on the Sabbath eve the old women light candles in the corner of the room.

Among the tribes of the region is a tribe calling itself "Afridi" – referring to the tribe of Ephraim, "Jaji" – referring to Gad, and "Lewani" – referring to Levi. One tribe calls itself "Shafe Mazhab", that is to say "religion in abundance", but I do not know its meaning. Another tribe is called "Shimoni", and they inhabit the area between the city of Maimana and Shibergan. Between the city of Aqucha and the city of Mazar lives the Malmuli tribe, most of whom are tent-dwelling nomads like the Ishmaelites. They had a tightly closed room that they feared to open. A Jew who happened to be in the area dared to open the door. Inside he found a scroll of the Law written on parchment, as is the Jewish custom.

When I was in Lahore in Punjab, now Pakistan, I entered into conversation with a Muslim, until we began to argue about religion. There was a young local man who heard the argument. He jumped up and told me: 'You, sir, be quiet, I will answer him!' He proceeded to bitterly attack the Muslim, and finished by saying: 'Mohammed is a lie and his law is a lie. Moses is true and his Law is true.' When I rose to return to my hotel, the young man approached me and told me that about 30,000 Jews live around the city of Habat Abad, between Lahore and Peshawar, today Pakistan. They live in special neighborhoods, like a ghetto. On Friday afternoon they close the gates of the ghetto, and they rest from all labor on the Sabbath. Disputes and judgments between them are arbitrated by the elders on the Sabbath in a large square, which is like a community center. There is a room there with a locked door that they are afraid to open. Each one kisses the door before he goes home. A transgressor, or one who approached a menstruating woman, is punished on the Sabbath. They tie him until evening to a column of shame erected beside the room. On Sabbath eve they light candles. They do not intermarry with people not of their tribe. They have their own special cemetery in which their dead are laid in the grave with the head towards the east and the feet towards the west. Also in the city of Jalandhar, between New Delhi and Ahmedabad, there is one tribe numbering a few thousand people who give their sons Biblical names, especially names of the Patriarchs and Matriarchs, and they light Sabbath candles."[9]

5) Testimony of Mr. Gabriel Borochov, a Bukharan Jew

I left Bukhara and traveled to the city of Andkhoi, and from there to Mazar and Kabul. Once I traveled with a friend to the Afghan mountains, to a place where the Afghan nomads live. We saw on the back of their clothes an embroidered pattern that was similar to a Hanukkah lamp with nine candles. They also had sidelocks on their cheeks. To my question – 'Who are you, what are your names?' they answered that they were 'Shabronis', 'Afridis' and 'Gadis'".

(Here Mr. Borochov added a comment): There is an Afghan Jew called Aba Koret, and he tells that when he was in Afghanistan he traveled with people of these tribes in a car, and found *mezuzot* tied to their hands, and that they were always covered with a blanket, like a *tallit* over their

9   From the booklet *Yeda Am* 4, 5.

clothes. When they pray they remove it and spread it before them. This they call 'Joy-namaz' – place of prayer. These tribes are wealthy, their wives are healthy and they have horses, sheep, cows, camels and mules.

They liked to ask questions about the Jews, and told me that on very Friday afternoon after the noon prayers their wives light candles, and that the women maintain their purity and immerse after their days of impurity in the sea or in pools.

I used to shave them, that is my profession, and I would have to be careful not to touch their mustaches or sidelocks. Most of them are bearded, and all have mustaches. They pray like all the gentiles (that is the Muslims). Their language is Persian-Afghan. They marry only among their tribes. They live near Kabul and Peshawar. They were interested in us and knew we were "Sons of Musa", but after some of the Jews among us started selling them *Arak* (alcohol), their friendly attitude changed, and they saw us as commercial competitors. Most live in dwellings made of upright straw, which is slanted and plastered on top. They use hunting rifles and knives, and go with caravans on pilgrimage to Mecca and Medina, but not to Karbala (so they are Sunni Muslims and not Shiites).

6) Testimony of Aba Koret of Tel Aviv

He used to spend four to five months a year in the tents of the various tribes, and he tells of things that he saw with his own eyes:

We used to buy wool from the Afridi and Shinwari tribes. They knew we were Jews and that we would not eat from the meat that they slaughtered. Their elders said that they were once Jews. One 90-year-old told me that he had heard from his father that they were Jews of the tribe of Shimon (Shinwari). They grow sidelocks and cover themselves with a long cloth over their clothes, similar to our *tzitzit*, although it lacks the fringes.

The head of the Afridi (Ephraim) tribe was Mohammed Khan Tarzi, and his tribe lived between Siaband and Kandahar.

Not all the women observed the custom of lighting candles, but four to five old women would light a small candle on Friday before evening, and say that it is some sort of "remembrance". Since they have no rooms, they light candles in a sort of courtyard where they keep a special box or case, and they do not do it publicly. Though the Afghans knew that it was Jews who came to buy wool from them, they never displayed any animosity towards us. This happened in the month of Kislev 5694 (1933-1934), when a decree was issued for the expulsion of 3000 Jews. The decree was actually against Bukharan and Russian Jews, but it affected all the Jews in the area, about 300 people.

7) Testimony of Abraham Ben Benjamin, formerly of Herat, arrived in Israel in 1951

The Afridis are the Sons of Israel by their own tradition, and they claim to be of the tribe of Ephraim. They grow sidelocks on both sides. The elders generally do not hide their origin, but a recent change has come over the youth, who have estranged themselves from their tradition because of foreign national influences.

According to my information there lives between Baluchistan and Kavita on the Indian side of the border the Lewani tribe, brave camel-riders numbering 10,000-20,000, who are said to be of the tribe of Benjamin. There are also the Vaslis, the Jajis who are said to be of Gad, and the Shinwaris – Shimon. In all, these tribes number half a million people. The Afridis live in the mountains; the famous among them are known as "Kosomengal" in their language. They are tall with black eyes and an eastern beauty in their faces. They are independent and do not accept foreign rule, not even the official rule of Afghanistan or India. Each tribe has a special leader called a "Malic", each with a special flag. In addition to the tribal leaders there are three main leaders who are absolute rulers of the tribes.

8) Testimony of Abraham Ben Agajan Hakohen (1951), leader of the Herat community, arrived in Israel in 1951

His father held a very influential post in the court of the king, Amir

Habibullah (Abi Amin Alla) but eventually met the same fate as many Afghani Jews – he was killed in Kabul by Muslim fanatics. Mr. Abraham Hakohen recalls that when he was a child he was present at a great feast that his father prepared in honor of the king, where he heard King Habibullah himself remark: "I am from the Benjamin tribe".

He also heard from Dr. Aga-Kahn: Abd a-Rahman, the father of Habib-Alla and the grandfather of Amin-Alla wrote in his article 'Afghanistan Tarikhi' that the Afghans are of Jewish origin and that they accepted Islam only in the Abbasid era in Iran and Persia.

Mr. Hakohen met the Afridi in the mountains, and they told him the following:

They heard from their elders that they are from the Jews. It is their custom that some of the old men or women light a candle on Friday towards evening. They have sidelocks on both cheeks opposite the earlobe, and they shave the remainder. They carry cloths like a Tallit that they wrap around themselves. When they pray they spread it out and bow down on it. It is called "Joy-namaz" (place of prayer) in Persian, but it has no threads that might recall our fringes (tzitzit). They eat from Jewish slaughtering, but will not eat from Shiite slaughtering. They will only marry within the tribe and not with strangers.

9) Testimony of Yehezkel Batzal (or Betzalel)

Mr. Betzalel visited me [Yitzhak Ben Zvi] with his friend Mr. Daniel Gul, head of the Afghan community in Jerusalem. He related the following:

The king rules the Afghans. In our time he was Dahir (Zahar) Khan Bin Nadir Shah. I was a merchant, and in the course of my work I traveled from Kabul to Peshawar by way of the mountains inhabited by the Afridi. From them I heard that they were Jews, of the tribe of Ephraim, the Jajis – Gad, and the Shinwari-Shimon. They have corners (like prayer shawls) on their clothes, and they grow sidelocks. Some families among them light candles on Friday evening after prayer, and they believe that if the candle goes out the soul will die within a year. There are also some who circumcise on the eighth day, unlike the Muslims who generally circumcise at a later age – though no later than 13 years.

They have one family, which has a private Mosque, which is a room, with a Menorah in it. They say that a sick person who looks upon the Menorah is cured.

Once when I was in Kabul, a gentile driver approached me, but did not speak when he saw that there were people with me. Another time he returned and came to me on the Sabbath. When he found that I was alone he asked to be taught Hebrew writing, and said: 'I am a Jew. We have many Jewish customs and I want to learn our writing. I am from the Sons of Josef ("Yusuf-Zai"). We are true Jews, but we fear to reveal our Judaism because of our neighbors. We live in Yagiashan in the mountains between Kabul and Peshawar, in the Khyber Pass'.

Their language is Pushtu. They live from agriculture, working their own fields (summer crops). Some worked for the British army, and today most are in the Pakistani army but not in the Indian army. They have mosques, and each family has a prayer area. They bring guests to the mosque to rest.

Jews do not come to them to do business, so they have no contact with Jews. In India they are called "Pathans" and in Afghanistan they are called "Pathan-ali". Mr. Betzalel once met a Muslim friend in Kandahar in Afghanistan, and the friend told him that he had encountered a few Pathans, and they asked him where he was going. When he told them "to Jerusalem the Holy City", they said: "one prayer said there (they said 'the Temple' – that is Jerusalem) is the equivalent of 1,000 prayers said here (in Afghanistan).

10) From the Memorandum of Mr. Hiya Zaorov, 1950, Tel Aviv

I had a discussion with the vizier of Afghanistan, Gulam Nebi Khan, and this is what I heard him say: 'The Afghans are descended from the sons of Israel from the time of the destruction of the First Temple, and especially the residents of the city of Kandahar near the capital Kabul. The royal dynasty there is all of Benjaminite descent. All of those tribes between Afghanistan and Peshawar who rise up periodically against England and other governments, and who accepted Islam, claim to be of Gad and Ephraim'.

11) Testimony of Yaakov Yitzhakov, 1957, former head of the Kabul community

The tribe of Ephraim – Afridis (who wear sidelocks), the tribe of Gad – Jaji, and the tribe of Shimon – Shinwari, all three number about 7 million. The Benjamin tribe is said to be related to the royal family.

[Yitzhakov visited the tribes on business.] The Afridis light candles for the Sabbath – a wick of cotton in oil – and leave it outside. They lend money with interest and smuggle goods. They are a nomadic people who live in the mountains between India and Afghanistan, in Pakistan and in Baluchistan and do not serve in the army. The Afridi are Muslims, have a mosque, go on the Haj and fast during Ramadan, but they are unlike other Sunni Muslims. Their clothes have fringes as a remembrance of a prayer shawl. They give alms among themselves and marry only within the tribes. Most are illiterate. They came in contact with Jews on business and trusted them.

The Lewani tribe is nomadic and lives in tents. The people dress in black and go to India for winter. Being nomads they do not work the land, and have sheep, cattle and camels. They trade with Jews. Their descent is unknown, but some of them also light Sabbath candles.

The Shinwari tribe works in commerce and transport. All carry arms. They grow sidelocks, but those of the Afridis are longer than theirs. The Shinwari have one synagogue in the village of Andra and one in Mulmul. Some of them circumcise their sons on the eighth day, but others are like the Muslims and circumcise their sons at 12-13 years.

Pathan is a name of derision to the Afghans, and was given to them by Jews. Among the tribes is a tribe called Yusuf Zai (Sons of Josef), and another called Musa Zai (Sons of Moses). All the tribes were forcibly converted to Islam.

12) Testimony of Menahem Levi, 1930

In January of 1930 at eight in the morning I left Hankin by wagon (litter). Before leaving, I was warned that it was a very bad time to travel, and by afternoon the mules sank up to their necks in the snow, and travel became impossible. 'We will go to the Hibur' said the driver. We walked almost seven hours before we reached the first tent. I was told that it was the tent of the sheikh, and when I entered he received me with great honor. As is my custom, I asked him: 'Do you know that I am a Jew?' 'I recognized your face and was glad of your coming' said the sheikh. He immediately brought me food and a chicken to slaughter. I slaughtered it, and he ate with us. I stayed with him for three days, and from discussions I learned of their life and ways. They believe in Mohammed, but admit to being descended from Jews of Hibur. On the ten days of Muharam they flagellate themselves more than others do, and it became their custom because their ancestors killed the holy ones, and they wish to be forgiven for their fathers' sins.

The name of the tribe is Kalataki, or the Tent of Kalta, and I was told they have 700 tents. Of Judaism they have only retained a few names, such as Shimon, Yakov, and Yosef, and strangely, they also have the name Akivah.

They have no education, and only perhaps five or six of the tribe can read. They live from the "hashab" (herds) and they change their grazing grounds four times a year. The government generally collects taxes from them, but they often rebel, especially when there is some change of the government.

Near Brojrad there are other similar tribes. Officially all are Muslim, but there are traces of Jewish customs.

13) Other Testimonies

a. The wise man Yosef Eliahu was imprisoned by the Hiwaris. He lived in the city of Balkh and came to Kabul on occasion. He also conducted business in the city of Mazar. He served as rabbi in Herat or Kabul.

He wrote about the customs of the Hiwari, but did not publish his writings. The Hiwari number 1,500-1,600. The women work the fields and the men raid the roads. Though he was their captive, they treated him with great respect. They do not adhere to ritual slaughtering, but when they pray they say, "Musa is G-d's prophet". They circumcise on the eighth day. They once had an ancient Torah Scroll, but the Bukharans took it from them and sold it to Baron Rothschild when he was in Bukhara. The casing was taken by the Bolsheviks and sent to the "Jewish section" of their museum in Moscow. They live in tents and caves in the mountains between Baluchistan, Afghanistan and Kave-Zar. They fast once a year (in remembrance of Yom Kippur, according to their date).

b. The Lewani number 10,000-20,000 brave, camel-riding warriors. They live between Baluchistan and Kavita, towards the Indian border. They are said to be of the tribe of Benjamin.

c. The tribes of Wazistan, on the borders of India, outside Afghanistan are close to the Afghan populations in language and traditions. The number of males of army age is 48,000, including 30,000 Whirling Dervishes and 18,000 Mahmudis.[10]

d. In addition to these warrior tribes, whose conversion to Islam predates the Arab conquests, there are several tribes and clans in Afghanistan, which were later forced to accept Islam, and these retained more traces of Jewish origin. A few examples are presented below:

1. Between the Afghan border and former Soviet Russia, in a place called Markau, lives the Musa-Zai family (sons of Moses). They too have customs like those found among the above-mentioned sons of Israel.

2. In the Maimana area near Andkhoi, 15 days out of Herat, is a clan called Malmal, whose sons were still Jewish 100 years ago, before being forcibly converted to Islam. The Malmal number about 1,000 families, who do not marry with the Muslims, but only among

---

10   Encyclopedia Britannica, vol. 18, p. 5.

themselves. The Muslims call them to this day "Jedid Al Islam" (newcomers to Islam), like the forced converts of the Mashhad, and this places their forced conversion at a later date than that of the Afridi.

3. According to a certain tradition, the Amir Nadir Shah of the Yusuf-Zai tribe received a Hebrew Bible and other holy objects, but did not know what they were. He asked a Jewish soldier serving in his legions about them, and the soldier recognized the artifacts and explained them to the king.

14) Testimony of Shmuel Shabtai, translated by Mordechai Zar, recorded by Yitzhak Ben-Zvi

In my article "The Afghanistan Tribes and the Tradition of their Origin from the Ten Tribes"[11], I [Yitzhak Ben Zvi] collected and recorded testimonies which I received from Jews who saw and heard at firsthand the popular traditions and legends of the Afghan tribes, especially among the Afridis, Duranis, Yusuf-Zai, Levi-Lewanis etc.

Now I have chanced upon Shmuel Shabtai Dadash, an immigrant from Afghanistan who arrived last year. He comes from Herat, but relates that he spent a few months as a merchant peddler among the wandering tribes in the Afghanistan and Baluchistan regions, especially among the Shinwari, Siabandar, and Afridi tribes. As such, he became acquainted with their way of life, and noticed their special customs that were reminiscent of Jewish ones. He also relates that he was jailed for 14 years in the central Kabul prison, where he came into close contact with members of these tribes who were also imprisoned there, and so gained additional knowledge of their customs.

The fact of the existence of a Jewish tradition among the Afghan tribes is not new. One can find material on the topic, and even a bibliography, in the Encyclopedia Britannica, under "Afghanistan". I have in my possession the Persian book "Taarikh I-Afgan", published in Teheran in

11   Davar Year Book, 1952, pp. 198-212.

the year 1321 of the Hegira. This book was written by Abd-A-Rahman Khan, the grandfather of Amanulla, and in it he recalls the tradition of their origin, especially that of the royal Afghan dynasty, from the Jews.[12]

The following report was written in Judeo-Persian by Shmuel Shabtai and translated by the learned Mordechai Zar. It contains more factual material of the way of life of the tribes and their legends, and though it was written from notes that he took down locally, it may be inexact. I am not responsible for the material, but it generally supports evidence that I collected from other sources, some of which I have published, and even adds to it. It is important to publish such correspondence written by eyewitnesses, and I have checked the validity of his testimony as closely as possible.

I feel that it is important to publish such testimonies in order for the public to be informed, and also in order to encourage immigrants from Afghanistan to come forward and provide us with additional information.

All this will aid researchers in the field to closely and scientifically check the facts regarding customs and traditions of the Afghan tribes.

(Yitzhak Ben Zvi, "The Dispersed of Israel")

Excerpts from "Beterem" – 1.1.1952

The border area of Afghanistan and Pakistan, called Pushtunistan, is inhabited by two million people claiming to be of Jewish origin and calling themselves Sons of Israel. Their borders are free and their land is called "Yakistan" (the rebels). They are completely independent, and have no representative outside their border. They see themselves as being of the 12 tribes descended from the Patriarch Jacob. They are very tall, with long noses and elongated faces, and have beards and sidelocks.

Their children also do not remove their sidelocks. On Sabbath eve they light candles and they have fringes-strings on the corners of their clothes. These are ancient customs that they keep. They consider themselves of

12   Part 2, p. 141.

Jewish stock, and if someone suggests to them that they are not Jews they get very angry and strongly insist upon their Jewishness. They belong to 12 large families (*hamoulas*), each considered to be one of the 12 tribes.

These families are:

The **"Rabbani" family**, i.e. Reuven. They live mainly in the mountain region, have herds of cattle and sheep, and are extremely hospitable.

The **"Shinwari" family**, i.e. Shimon, has customs that are completely different from those of the Rabbanis. Each family lives on its own clearly defined boundary.

The **"Lewani" family**, i.e. Levi, is aristocratic. They have many judges and notables. They are wealthy and trade on the Indo-Kush border.

The **"Yunim" family**, i.e. Judah, rules all 12 tribes together, and is especially respected by the others. "Yunim" and "Lewani" are known in all Afghanistan and are recognized as honored and aristocratic.

The **Yitsaki family** engages primarily in grazing. Their elders teach religion to the other families.

The **"Jaji" family**, i.e. Zebulon, are farmers, and most of them are also craftsmen and drivers. Transport between India and Afghanistan is mostly in their hands.

The **"Zai-Khan" family**, i.e. Naftali (Zai in Afghan means family). The most aristocratic branch among them is that of Mohammed Zai. This family is dispersed along the borders of the country. The **Durani family** is also well known in all Afghanistan. In the book "The History of Afghanistan", written by the Afghan minister of education, Mohammed Naim Khan, the Durani family is reported to be of Jewish descent. The Mohammed Zai and Durani families are large families, well-known throughout Afghanistan.

The **"Kaka Khil" family** is Gad (the David family). They are known as peasants and farmers, and dwell in the mountain regions.

The **"Azhik Zai" family** – Asher, lives between Kandahar and Kabul. It is a well-known merchant family. They are known by their yellow beards, wide eyebrows and long faces.

The **"Mumand" family** – that is Menashe, is large and well known. The Afghan war minister of a few years ago, Gul Mohammed Khan, was of this family.

The **"Afridi" family,** i.e. Ephraim, is well known among the Jews, and the English. During World War I, the English drafted many of them into their army. They are known as good warriors, all carry arms, and they even manufacture arms. There are numerous legends about their bravery.

There are other well-known families, such as "Suleiman Khil", "David Zai", "Yusuf-Zai" and others, in all about 2 million people.

It is known among the 12 families that their forefathers were scattered in the mountains with no spiritual leader until Mohammed came and forced his religion on them. However, it did not alter their belief in their Jewish origin or the observance of the Jewish customs.

For 2,000 years they did not forget their origin and their roots in the Patriarch Jacob, and so they retained their separateness and independence. Unlike the Muslims, their wives do not cover their faces, and work in agriculture and shepherding. They know how to work and fight, and teach their children how to use weapons. They circumcise their sons up to the age of five or six. During the eighteen years that I lived among them, I grew to know all their customs. They are very happy to meet Jews, but because they dwell far from the Afghan Jews their contact is limited and they developed a language called Pushtu.

When the British left these countries, India and Pakistan declared their independence and both Pakistan and Afghanistan sought to include these families in their borders and count them among their citizens. Family leaders were invited and bribed and were even offered their own state, Pushtunistan, under Afghan protection. Afghans claimed that the tribes were of Afghan stock and that their language is Afghani. Pakistan on the other hand, claimed that they lack education and culture, which she can offer them, as well as teaching them modern agriculture, etc. They offered them a few million rupees per year to use as they saw fit and enable them to be independent. There is therefore a constant dispute between Pakistan and Afghanistan over these tribes.

About 98% of the tribes are illiterate. They know how to pray and they fast during the month of Ramadan. They wear long cloaks, very wide pants made of white cloth, cloth belts, and turbans on their heads. They are physically very healthy and immune from disease. I personally saw a woman hurrying down to the spring. On the way she went into labor. She gave birth on her own, picked up the baby and returned to the tent with a full pitcher of water. There are many such examples. The people of the tribes are very health and strong. They are hard working and their main occupation is agriculture and shepherding. The English fought for many years and suffered many losses in trying to make these tribes part of India in order to stabilize the borders, but the bravery and stubbornness of the families kept them free, and to this day they accept citizenship from no country.

Their law is similar to written Jewish law: a life for a life, an arm for an arm, and a strictly enforced law of damages – an identical damage in retribution for a damage inflicted. They are always armed, as are their children and wives. They have a custom that in the case of a murder, the murderer must pay the family of the victim the sum of 10,000 Afghan rupees and a young girl.

They consider themselves in exile and have little contact with the outside world. Some have heard about the establishment of the State of Israel and the Israeli government, and they wish to come and see it personally.

Testimonies Collected by Avraham Zonenshein
(From his book "New Light in Zion")

1) Testimony of Mr. Agagan Abramov Shemesh

The following is what I was told by Mr. Agagan Abramov Shemesh, a 100-year-old Afghan immigrant, may G-d give him long life, who lives in Tel Aviv.

All the names ending in Khan, such as Abdul Khan or Rahman Khan, are of the same family and are our brothers who were forced to accept another religion. They were still Jews three hundred years ago. Ala Bangivan, a summer resort village, is populated by forced converts to Islam. All the following testimonies regarding the origin and conversion of our brothers – Jajis (Gad), Shinwaris, Afritis – were verified by Mr. Agagan, and he told me that the information was learned incidentally during meetings with the tribes. Had the purpose of the meetings been research, much more information could have been obtained.

2) Testimony of Avraham Abulof

A resident of one of the Jaji villages around Kabul once visited the Jewish *Hakham* (wise man) of the Bukharan community in Kabul. During their conversation the Hakham noticed that the Jaji was holding an amulet of leather. He became curious and questioned him about the amulet, but the Jaji could not tell him what it was or what it contained. The Hakham then asked permission to open the amulet. The Jaji adamantly refused, explaining that opening the amulet was grounds for excommunication, and that one who dares to ignore this tradition will go blind. The Hakham insisted and by various enticements succeeded in opening the amulet. To his great astonishment, he found the first verse of "Shema Yisrael" (Hear O Israel) written in clear Hebrew script.

3) Mr. Zevulun Kort, a Bukharan, member of "Davar" newspaper editorial board, of Tel Aviv

In the matter of the amulets commonly found among the Jaji, a friend of mine who was a peddler traveling in the Afghan hills once spent a night in one of the Jaji villages. In the evening he was invited to a family, and there were other villagers present. They all had amulets and told him it was a tribal custom, and that it provided the holder of the amulet with special protection from evil. He questioned them about the contents of the amulets and finally, overriding protests, managed to open one. What he found inside was the first verse of "Shema Yisrael". He was told that only one man in the tribe knows how to write such an amulet, and the skill and knowledge is passed from father to eldest son. The writer is considered a holy man, and he writes the amulets in a special room within a room.

Once a Jewish peddler arrived at a distant village, and entered its inn, the Tchahina (Tea House). The inn keeper knew that a Jew would not eat his food, so he supplied him with fruit, vegetables, eggs and milk. The peddler had his own teapot, so the inn keeper filled it with tea, and the Jew dipped his bread in tea and ate. A Shiite then entered, saw the Jew eating alone, and called to the other Muslims sitting there: 'See that impure Jew, afraid to touch our food which he sees as impure. You see your shame and remain quiet?' The mob wanted to attack the Jew and kill him. However, one of the notables of the community was there, said to be a descendant of the Ten Tribes, and he said to the inciter: 'Are you a Sunni? You are a Shiite!' (The Sunnis hate the Shiites and are even prepared to kill them.) 'Do you know who a Jew is? It is to the Jews that G-d chose to give His Torah. Their leader was Moses, G-d's servant. And who are you, Shiite? An infidel and a son of an infidel, a dog and a son of a dog! The Jew is pure in body and in his food, and does not eat impure food like you, and what have you to make an outcry about?' Since then they honored the peddler. Each sent him a gift and wanted to have the peddler stay with him.

Yohai Eliav told me: "During the Israeli War of Independence in 1948, my neighbor in Kabul, an owner of a fabric store and a Jew-hater told me:

The Arabs are fighting the Jews and will destroy them in one more week. I was afraid to answer him fearing that he might libel me, saying that I cursed Mohammed. A second neighbor, a learned and wise man, told me: "Look, your Jews in the Temple make problems". However, I continued to remain silent. Some time later, I again entered the store, and the owner turned and said to me: "If the Jews win in the wars with the Arabs I will convert". A year later, when the battles ceased in Israel, I entered that same store, and my neighbor said to me: "I am ready to convert but I cannot do it here – zealots will kill me. Take me to Jerusalem and there I will convert".

4) Testimony of Mr. Yehezkel Batzal (Betzaleli), of Tel Aviv

Among the bravest of the Afriti families in Afghanistan is the Yusuf-Zai (Sons of Josef) family. During World War I, two of their soldiers served with the British in Palestine, camping near Hadera. They sought out Afghan Jews in Palestine, asking them to send a special rabbi to Afghanistan to teach their tribe Jewish laws. The request of the two soldiers was not granted for some reason and no group was sent to teach the tribe. Mr. Batzal noted what a pity it was that the community did not realize the importance of the matter. In his testimony to Mr. Ben Zvi, Mr. Batzal, told also of a driver of the Yussuf-Zai tribe who visited him while he was still in Afghanistan, and asked to be taught Jewish writing. He said about his tribe: 'We are true Jews, but we fear our neighbors and so do not disclose our Judaism'.

In 1958, when we were on our way to Israel by way of India, we reached the Indian border (Pakistan today) on a Sunday. The British office at the crossing station refused to stamp our passports on the official day of rest. This distressed us greatly, for we feared that the Afghan government might change its mind at the last minute and revoke our exit permits, so we tried to persuade the office to stamp our passports, and the elderly among us entreated him. The officer then asked us where we were going from India. When we answered that we were going to Jerusalem he was taken aback and asked again: "To Jerusalem?", and he asked in English if the Wailing Wall was there. When the elders answered: yes, he immediately stamped all the passports. When he finished he turned to the elders and made the following request: 'When you arrive at the Wailing Wall (Kotel) say a prayer for me also, for I am also of the seed of the Jews. I am from Punjab (Pakistan), and please ask G-d to return His lost sons'. And we the elders saw tears in the officer's eyes.

5) Testimony of Mr. Simantov Sasson, of Tel Aviv

During my work among the Afghan immigrants for the Department of Immigration of Middle East Jews I had discussions with immigrants and discovered the following facts:

Beyond the high mountains in the Khyber Pass, in the Pathan region of Afghanistan, which borders on Pakistan at the end of the Iranian heights connecting the Middle and Far East, there dwells a tribe known as the Levoni. This tribe calls itself "sons of Israel", and claims to be related to the tribe of Benjamin. The people of the tribe are healthy, immune to disease and are known as brave fighters, having participated in the many recent wars fought between the Afghan and Pakistani tribes. By law they are under the protection of the Afghan Sultan and must obey the royal house, but in practice they are independent and have local autonomy. Afghan authorities do not dare to provoke them, because this might start a tribal rebellion costing the Afghan army many casualties. The men of the tribe all carry arms despite the law against it, and they even manufacture arms. The English pay them high wages to act as a garrison force, especially in India and its surrounding areas.

They have a number of customs that point to their Jewish origin. They have Hebrew names, wear a four-cornered tallit from the age of 13, light candles on Sabbath eve – and then hide the candles, grow sidelocks and beards, and circumcise the boys on the eighth day. One of the cities of the tribe has a house called "The Holy House". The house is surrounded in mystery and is tightly shut. An ancient ancestral custom of protecting it from all evil prohibits anyone from approaching it. One of the elders of the tribe revealed that the house is a synagogue and that it contained Torah Scrolls. When the existence of the scrolls became known to Afghan Jews, they sent a group of community representatives to negotiate the acquisition of the scrolls for a great deal of money. However, the people of the tribe refused to part with the scrolls, claiming that it is a possession proving their belonging to the tribe of Israel, that it was passed down the many generations from ancient ancestors who warned them not to touch the scrolls. In times of danger and tribulation, all the people of the tribe gather around the synagogue, cry and pray until the evil passes.

Aside from serving as soldiers in various armies, some of the people are talented merchants who live by transporting goods from the Near East to the Far East, and levying a road tax from caravans passing through their regions. The members of the tribe also understand and befriend the Afghan Jewish community. One of the regional officers of the city of Herat was of this tribe. He was in charge of stamping exit visas for people traveling from Herat, among them of Jews traveling from Herat to Mashhad. When visited by a Jewish community dignitary regarding the preparation of travel papers, he asked the dignitary the destination of the Jews who were traveling from Herat. When he was answered that they were traveling to the Land of Israel, the officer exclaimed: 'I am of the Children of Israel – why are you going to Israel?'

There are other tribes of Jewish origin in the region, for instance the tribe of Shimon, known locally as the Shinwari, and the tribe of Gad, called Jaji.

The national museum in Kabul displays a very ancient stone found in an excavation near the city, and written on it in Hebrew letters is a tale of a vicious pogrom against the tribes of the area. It tells of a rebellion of the youth of the tribe against being forced to convert, and of their being slaughtered in battle. The stone is their memorial.

6) Testimony of Mr. Hanimof Gavriel, of Tel Aviv

As a merchant traveling and selling clothes to villagers in Afghanistan, I came into close contact with the people of these tribes, said to be descendants of the lost Jewish tribes. They always received us with warmth and love, and called us Mishia (Moshe in the Pushtu language). In every city or village in which the Mukhtar was a member of one of the tribes, we were treated well and allowed to sell as much as we wanted. However, if the Mukhtar was an Indian he made problems for us. As a professional barber, when giving them haircuts I was warned by them not to touch their beards or sidelocks. When asked why, they answered that it is an ancient custom, and that under no circumstances will they depart from the tradition of their fathers.

It happened that one of the Jaji went frequently to Kabul on business, and the British bureaucrats often made fun of his beard and sidelocks and called him Jewish. Once they overdid it and upset him so much that in his anger he entered a barbershop and had his beard and sidelocks removed. However, he had cause to regret his action, because when he returned to his village, he was chased away for disregarding their customs and traditions, and he found himself in a very embarrassing situation indeed. He had no choice but to grow his beard and sidelocks anew.

7) Testimony of Mr. Yakov Danieli, of Tel Aviv

I know the lost tribes well. I worked in their region many times. It is known that in Kings II 17:6 it is written concerning the exile of the Ten Tribes, that the king of Assyria settled them in Halat, and Hibur and the Gozan River. Because I examined closely places settled by the tribes and I know well the language of the land, I know that the Gozan River is Rud Jazan – 'Rud' is the word for 'river' in their language. The Gozan River flows from the Kandahar region in Afghanistan to the Karachi region of Pakistan. On both sides and along the entire length of the river live our brothers of the lost Sons of Israel. I met them in their multitudes on both banks of the river, from the Shinwari tribe – supposedly of Shimon, to the Afridati and Rabbani (Reuven). On the Pakistani side the Biblical Hibur is located. It is undoubtedly Peshawar. In the local language it is pronounced Peshhibur.

About 30 years ago, I once traveled with one of my children by the

Gozan River in the region of our tribes. The child had sidelocks, and as
we passed by one village, we were suddenly set upon by many people of
the tribe who wanted to kill me. When I succeeded by a miracle in calming
them a little and asked why they had attacked me, they explained that it
was clear to them that I had kidnapped the child from their region, for to
grow sidelocks is only the custom of the sons of the tribe, who are the
Sons of Israel, and only they grow sidelocks.

8) Testimony of Amnon Eliav

When I was in Kabul and Kandahar, I met inhabitants of the surrounding villages who considered themselves descendants of Israel,
remnants of the Ten Tribes. In the village of Nuristan, the men wear "four
corners" over their clothes, though without fringes, and they have a
tradition from the village elders that he who wears "four corners" will not
be hurt in battle, and bullets will not pierce his body.

In Chaghcharan an ancient stone was founded in 1947, on which were
engraved Hebrew letters. The stone aroused archeological interest, and
was taken to the Dar-El-Amman museum in Kabul. The same region has
a large Jewish grave, with a prayer house beside it. I arrived one Sabbath
eve at one of the villages of the Afridi tribe, and stayed there in a Muslim
home. How astonished I was when they lit candles and hid them in a
corner of the house! I was told it was a remnant of an ancient custom, but
they could not explain what it was. On the Sabbath eve they served grape
juice to members of the family, although Muslim law forbids drinking
juice of the vine, but they will not give up their old tradition. Once an old
woman returned from the mosque on Yom Ha-Mamia (Friday) and
recounted that the sheikh had told them in a sermon that the Jews had
conquered all of Palestine, and control the Temple, and all the cities. If
so, she said, "Islam is false and we should all convert".

9) Testimony of Mr. Mikhael Bar Yosef, an elder of the Bukharan community

In 1948, after the establishment of the State of Israel, I was still in the city of Kabul in the exile of Afghanistan. When we heard of the establishment of the State, our joy knew no bounds and many of our Bukharan brothers decided to immigrate to Israel. It was not easy to do so, however, because Afghanistan was zealously Muslim and would not easily grant exit visas to Jews, especially during the War of Independence, when it was considered reinforcements for the Jews. At that time I sat in a Muslim coffee house in Kabul, reading about Arab defeat and the loss of the cities of Lod and Ramle in an article appearing in a local newspaper. There were three Afghan officers in the coffee house. One of them said to me: 'I always thought that the Jews were cowards and the Arabs brave like us, and now I was surprised to hear the opposite. How do your Jews win?' At first I hesitated, deciding whether to answer them, but then all at once I became brave and said: 'You are wrong if you think the Arabs are brave, for they were never brave like you. They are cowards, and you only have the Muslim religion in common with them, because you are not of Arab stock but of Jewish stock, and you received your religion at a later date'. Hearing my answer, two of the officers became very angry, but the third one silenced them, saying: 'Why are you getting heated up? This Jew speaks the truth. I myself heard my father say that we are Afghans descended from the Tribes of Israel.' Then the officer beside him said: "If we are truly of Jewish stock, the Jews are our relations and brothers, and we should help them against the Arabs'.

These same officers later helped me get my emigration papers.

(Avraham Zonenshein, "New Light in Zion")

Testimonies collected by A. Bryn and E. Avichail

1) Testimony of Mr. Yitzhak Betzalel, of Ramat Gan

Afghanistan itself has about 15 million inhabitants. Some four million are Duranis, including the royal family, and they are more educated than the rest of the tribes. There are about six million Ghilzai, and also Uzbeks and Tajiks, people of Bukhara, principally on the Russian border. All the Afghans are Sunni Muslims except for about three million Shiites in the mountain regions in the center of the country. Basically, the Shiites hate the Jews. Such hatred is less evident among the Sunnis. There is enmity between the two Muslim sects. The Pathans are a people located in the Shamsin (Tibet) regions and all the way to Persia, but mostly in Pakistan along the border with Afghanistan. The capital of the Pathans is Pesh-Hibur (that is how he pronounces Peshawar). Pathan is a name given to them by the English. The Pathans number about eight million. They are fierce warriors and make up 80% of the Pakistani army. The English succeeded in laying a road in their region after paying a large sum of money. The Pathans are very aggressive and dangerous. Sometimes they kill all who stray from the road and do not travel on the main road. There are tribes among them that are said to be of the Ten Tribes.

The great majority of the Jews now living in Afghanistan came from Persia, and some are from among the forced converts of the Mashhad; 130 years ago pogroms were launched against the Mashhad Jews forcing them to accept Islam, and some then fled to Afghanistan. Mr. Betzalel's grandfather was among those who fled. In his opinion, all the Jews of Afghanistan accepted Islam 700 years ago and the present Afghan Jews are from Persia. Today most have immigrated to Israel, and those who remain in Afghanistan are protected by the king and his son.

About the tribes he told us the following: There is a nomadic tribe called Kuchi, found in winter in Pakistan and in the summer in Afghanistan. They pass Kabul on their way, and this is where Mr. Betzalel encountered them. They live in black goatskin tents and the women also wear black (he sees this as a sign of mourning for the destruction of the Temple in Jerusalem; here there may be a reference to the sons of Rehab, whom Jeremiah told to drink wine [Chapter 35], and they answered him that they do not drink and they sit all their days in tents). The tribe numbers over 20,000. The tribesmen have rifles and do not fear to use them at will.

Most of the Pathans have sidelocks and beards; all the Afridis have beards. Some of the Pathan children have strings on their clothes like a small tallit. The Pathan tribes that he feels are descended from the Ten Tribes are Afridis-Ephraim, Lewani-Levites, Rabbani-Reuven, Shinwari-Shimon, Daftani-Naftali and Jajis-Gad, all living in the PeshHibur area.

The Duranis are also considered to be of the Ten Tribes and also some of the Ghilzai. The royal family has a family tree all the way back to Benjamin the son of Jacob, and the tree also includes King Saul. The royal family and the king, who has learned the history of his people and has a large library and museum, claim that the Afghans are descended from the Ten Tribes. Yitzhak Betzalel adds that the king takes the most important archeological finds to his private museum, and perhaps for this reason he has proof of Afghan origins. The entire royal family is favorably inclined toward the Jews. There was a prince called Nabob Mardan who built a city and named its streets after cities in Israel. He also had a large library and liked the Jews. The name of the present king, who studied in France, is Zair Khan.

Every tribe has a few elders who remember the tradition and claim a connection to the Jews. However, the young people deny this and even become angry when they are told that they are Jews. The learned of the population also know that the Afghans are Jews. A Jew heard an old man who was a former prime minister claim before the present Prime Minister that they were Jews and not Aryans as claimed by modern authors. The Prime Minister said that he was right.

Mr. Betzalel had a store in Kandahar where he and his son sold cloth. One day a tall youth from a village between Kandahar and Kabul came in and started buying there regularly. Once he came in and said that his

80-year-old father asked from what nation they were. Mr. Betzalel answered him that they are Jews. The youth did not know what Jews were, and so Mr. Betzalel added: "Sons of Israel", the people of "Hazarat Musa". Some time later the youth came to their home and said that he came only to tell them that when his father heard that they were Jews, he said – "we are also Jews", and added that his father had a very large library and sat and learned all day. His father begged Mr. Betzalel to visit him in the village, but Mr. Betzalel refused because of the dangers of travel.

Regarding the verse in Kings II 17:6 which mentions that the Sons of Israel were exiled to "Halat, Hibur, Gozan River and the cities of Medes", and in the corresponding verse in Chronicles which mentions Hara instead of cities of Medes, Mr. Betzalel told me that Herat is called Hara in Afghanistan and that the elders call PeshHibur Pehibur. Mr. Betzalel feels this may be a corruption of Peh-Hibur. The Gozan River is the river Rud Jazan passing through northern Afghanistan It has 48 tributaries and flows into the Amu Darya, part of which makes up the border between Afghanistan and Russia. The river Rud Jazan passes by the cities Aqucha, Shibergan, Andkhoi, Maimana and Balkh. 'River' is 'Rud' in Persian.

The city of Balkh itself is very old and Megillat Esther was read here on the 15th of Adar (Shushan Purim). A large palace, extending over six kilometers, is situated there. The inhabitants do not know when they settled there, but there are some hidden history books on the subject. In Balkh, thousands of books were buried under 10 meters of earth and a road was built on top to keep them buried. Nearby is a place called Tashurgan (in the local language – small stone), which is east of Balkh and north of Mulmul on the Russian border. There were four to five families of hide merchants who had a synagogue and a ritual bath there. The synagogue had an ancient Torah scroll with crooked Hebrew letters, which are not like regular letters. Mr. Betzalel saw the scroll but did not want to take it, fearing that he would not be able to protect its holiness on the way to Israel. A Bukharan Jew took the scroll to Israel and sold it here. Finally it was taken to America and found to have been written by Ezra the Scribe.

Jews have lived in Maimana for 1,000 years. There is a village there called Musa and its inhabitants are said to have been Jews once. In the Balkh region is a place called Mulmul. Four hundred years ago there were 500 Jewish families there who were converted to Islam by force, their sheikh recounts. They only married among themselves. The king's son-in-law was a friend of the sheikh and he asked him to open the old synagogue of the village (the sheikh related that there was an old synagogue there in a cave covered with stones), but he adamantly refused.

Mr. Yitzhak Betzalel thinks it likely that the exiled sons of Israel arrived first at Herat-Hara and from there some continued to Gur-Sahar and the others to the Balkh area in North Afghanistan.

(Compiled by A. Brin, 1974)

2) Testimony of Mr. Lider, of Jerusalem

Mr. Lider traveled recently to Afghanistan by way of Iran. He stayed with a Persian Rabbi, who asked him why he was traveling to Afghanistan. When he answered that he sought lost Jews, the Rabbi told him that the tribe of Ephraim, called Afridi, was to be found in Afghanistan.

On the eve of the Passover, he approached a man who spoke Russian (the language spoken by Mr. Lider) in Kabul, and asked him about the Jewish tribes. The man said that there were two tribes – Afridi and Jaji, the Jaji tribe live in Jalalabad. He also told him of special customs found among the tribes, such as amulets with a verse of Shema Yisrael, and of lighting candles on Sabbath eve. He heard that the Afridi number 15 million. They do not marry with the other tribes. When a youth wants to marry, his parents go to the bride's parents. If the bride agrees, she is bought with the price determined according to her lineage. A bride cannot choose a groom, although she may send her friends to the boy's father. Jews at the Palace Hotel told him that the tribes have been in Afghanistan for more than 3,000 years. They are strictly religious and categorically refuse to be called Jews. The American consulate warned

Mr. Lider against remaining in the area of the nomadic tribes, but the Afridi tribe was peaceful at the time.

(Compiled by A. Brin, 1974)

3) Testimony of Mr. Meir Hai Ajajan

Mr. Ajajan came to Israel 40 years ago from Balkh in Afghanistan.

Most of the Pathans shave their heads and beards and leave their sidelocks unshaven. They consider the sidelocks holy and swear by them. Sabbath candles are found almost in every home. Their garment is open at the bottom on both sides up to about a third of the length, thus forming a four-cornered garment. A string is sewn to the corner. Fringes are found among almost all the Pathans, and amulets are commonly used by them and are kept in a silver case. They believe in it and in its power. These tribes resemble Jews in their appearance, and are intelligent and strong. In Mr. Ajajan's opinion they have no tradition regarding their origin, but other Jews told him that they heard on the train from a few Pathans that they are also lost Jews. From this he concludes that some Pathans know of their origin. Among the Jews it is clear that the Pathans are Jews. They all live in Pakistan in the PeshHibur region and together they number about one million people. They are very hospitable despite their fierceness.

The members of the royal family, called the Mohammed Zai, see themselves as being of the tribe of Benjamin, not necessarily descended from Saul. They are sympathetic towards Israel. They are a small tribe inhabiting the Kabul region but have no special customs reminiscent of their having been Jews.

The Lewanis live in the Balkh region – Mazar (Turkistan), an area that the Afghans did not conquer, and which was not formerly held by them. Mr. Ajajan thinks they have no Jewish origin.

(Compiled by A. Brin, 1974)

4) Testimony of Mr. Hiya Zaorov, of Tel Aviv

Mr. Zaorov came to Israel from Bukhara in 1935 and lives in Tel Aviv. He told me about the Afghan royal family.

When Gulam Nabi Khan, an Afghan minister, was in Tashkent, Mr. Zaorov spoke with him and was told of his royal family background and its descent from the tribe of Benjamin. They call themselves the 'Benjamin family', and there are some who call themselves 'sons of Benjamin'. He added that in the Peshawar region of Pakistan there were tribes descended from the Ten Tribes. The royal family is proud of its Jewish origin (but perhaps only in front of Jews). They honor the Jews and did so also in the past.

Aminulla Khan was king until 1928. His father Habibula Khan, when the Jews came to bless him on his coronation day, showed them his lineage from the sons of Benjamin. When Habibula's son wanted to reform the Afghan constitution, he requested of the Jews their books of personal and monetary laws in order to use them as a model in establishing his reforms. Mr. Zaorov felt that the king was trying in this way to reestablish the original Afghan constitution – the Law of Israel. Mr. Zaorov was told by his father, who was born in 1840, that Nadir Shah, who conquered part of Afghanistan over 100 years earlier, also requested of the Jews of his time that they translate their laws to aid him in administering his country. Nadir Shah, despite being a Persian king, was a Sunni and not a Shiite and he also liked the Jews. Nadir Khan, the former ambassador to France, became king after Aminulla Khan. While still ambassador, he would often discuss matters with and be advised by a Bukharan Jew – Eliyahu Yissakhar Khan (Yissakharov). After his coronation he called upon Eliyahu Yissakhar to join him in Afghanistan, where he was given a powerful and influential position in the palace. With Eliyahu's help many Bukharan and Afghan Jews came to Israel.

When Nadir Khan was murdered, an Afghan consul was sent to Mr. Hiya Zaorov in Bukhara to inform him that they were writing a book of condolences for the royal family, and to request the signatures of the Jews of Bukhara in Hebrew.

Mr. Hiya Zaorov also related that when the Bolsheviks took power in Russia, they divided the large area of South-Central Russia into smaller regions such as Tajikistan, Turkmenistan and Kazakhstan. In Tajikistan, which is north of Afghanistan, there was a village called Dushma and when Stalin rose to power he renamed it Stalinabad, and it began to develop and grow. Consequently, many Jews streamed to Tajikistan. They found that the Tajiks light candles on the Sabbath eve. Also when they came to visit with them they found that the Tajiks eat a meat and rice dish called "Bahash", which is specifically characteristic of the Bukharan Jews, and is eaten on Sabbath eve. When asked, "What is it?" the Tajiks answered that it was an old traditional dish, and they also related that they have a tradition that they were once Jews.

Rabbi Saadiah Gaon argued at length with the wise man Hivi of Balkh, and Mr. Zaorov feels that in Hivi's time the Jews tended to assimilate to Islam, and this is what their discussions were about.

The learned Ibn Sina of Bukhara also lived in that period. A Tajik teacher said that Ibn Sina was from the Jews, forcibly converted to Islam and called Chela. Also, the meaning of his name according to Mr. Zaorov is Son of Sinai (today in many languages, including Arabic, Sinai is pronounced Sin or Sina), and it is likely that he called himself Son of Sinai, meaning son of the Law that came from Sinai.

The Maharajah of Mardan was a scholar who had studied at university in London. He often met the forced converts of the Mashhad who lived in Peshawar. He also used to visit a Jew called Carmely, who told Mr. Zaorov that the Maharajah would always say that one day the origins of all men would be known and then it would be known that all the people of the Afghanistan region were once Jews. The Maharajah published a book in English and wrote of this in its introduction, but the book was lost. Mr. Zaorov, together with the deceased former President Yitzhak Ben Zvi, who thought the matter very important, had attempted unsuccessfully to find the book.

Some of the Bukharan Jews have a tradition that they are descended of people of the First Temple Period (perhaps of the Ten Tribes – but this was not known to him) and afterwards were joined by Jews of the Second Temple dispersion.

The Bukharans have a tradition that the Amu Darya River is the Gozan River. Mr. Zaorov saw in translation Rabbi Saadiah Gaon's Tafsir on the Bible (in Arabic) that translated Gozan as Balkh.[13] Mr. Zaorov estimates that the conversion of the tribes to Israel was at the time of Rabbi Saadiah Gaon and Hivi of Balkh.

(Compiled by A. Brin, 1974)

5) Testimony of Mr. Abraham Katanov, of Balkh, 1973

Mr. Abraham Katanov related the following facts to me:

1. The old women of all the tribes living in the Pakistan-Afghanistan border area light candles on the Sabbath eve.
2. All the tribesmen have sidelocks above their ears. Some also have beards, but these are not compulsory.
3. All wear a large cloak resembling a tallit without fringes, obligatory from the age of five.
4. One of these tribes is that of the "Suleiman Khil", living in the Suleiman Mountains in Pakistan.
5. The tribes marry only among themselves, namely one of the Jaji tribe can marry one of the Afridi tribes, but they do not marry strangers.
6. They have Hebrew names like Suleiman, Yakov, Ibrahim or Isak.
7. The tribal elders say that they are the Sons of Jacob, but they cannot differentiate and say to which tribe they belong.
8. Altogether these tribes number above one million people. They live in the border region between Pakistan and Afghanistan, in the Khyber Pass area. Mr. Katanov does not know anything the tribes of Baluchistan (further south). Until recently they were nomadic, but now the government is beginning to give them parcels of land in the Balkh region, so that they will settle permanently.

---

13   The author of this book also saw the translation.

9. In Mulmul there was forced conversion about 200 yeas ago. Until today there is a synagogue there with a ritual bath. About 120 families of Jews lived at the bottom of the mountain (they now live as gentiles). The non-Jews who forced the Jews to convert belonged to the Zakh and Polad families. Some of the forced converts fled, but others stayed, and to this day they only marry among themselves.

10. The royal family is called Yusuf Zai. Its other name is Binyamin Khil (Khil = tribe). The tradition is well known among them, and even the young announce proudly that they are of Jewish origin. They do not marry strangers, including the people of the border tribes.

(Compiled by A. Brin, 1974)

6) Testimony of Mr. Zevulun Kort, 1973

My friend Daniel Zeevi of Balkh told me about Jaji amulets. He was traveling in a remote, hardly accessible area and arrived around evening at a Jaji village in the Mangal region. There he saw some children aged 3-5 who wore amulets sewn into pouches around their necks. He took one of the amulets from one of them, opened it and found written in Assyrian script on rough paper the two words "Shema Yisrael" from the first verse of the "Hear O Israel", found in our Torah Scrolls. When he asked the adults about the amulet, they told him that a tribal leader writes the amulet and only he knows the secret of its writing. When he writes the amulet he sits near ashes (or in ashes). During his life he teaches the writing to his son and when he dies the son takes his father's place. When Daniel wanted to see the tribal leader and bless him, they refused to let Daniel see him and said it was forbidden to do so. They told him that every baby wears the amulet from birth. The host further said that they know that they are Jews.

Another time Daniel Zeevi went to the British Embassy, housed outside the walls of Kabul in the suburbs of the city. When he passed in one of the streets, children attacked him and began to hit him. When he called for help an old man came out from one of the houses, reprimanded the children and chased them away. When Daniel told him that he was going to the British Embassy to get a visa to travel abroad, the old man told him: 'I know where you are going – to the land of Israel – because I am also a Jew'. The old man asked him to pray for him when he arrived in Jerusalem.

Meir Khafi told me that he traveled from Kabul to Peshawar. On the way, in one of the villages, a householder met him and invited him into his home. It was the Sabbath eve and Meir saw on the table 12 loaves of bread, and his host told him that it was their tradition. In the corner he saw a lit candle covered by a basket.

According to legend, some of the Babylonian exiles looked for a better place, and they reached what is today Kabul, the capital of Afghanistan. The name means Land of Swamps, a good place for grazing, and a large river passes through the city. When they arrived, the local population accepted them with great honor, for they were majestic people, strong and tall. The exiled Jews became their Mukhtars and leaders, and after a while also their kings.

While Mula Avraham Kohen was staying in Kabul with the king, who honored him, they often talked, and the king would always say that he was a Jew. Once Mr. Avraham asked him: If you are a Jew why do you not act like the Jews, and why do you not leave Islam? The king answered: **It is a tradition from our elders; when the Messiah comes we will return to our Judaism,** as it is written (Genesis 40:10): 'Until Shilo comes, and unto him shall the obedience of the peoples be.'

Early on a winter morning in 1924, Rabbi Reuven Betzalel (Rabbi of the Afghan Jews in Tel Aviv) bought firewood. He urged the Ghilzai donkey driver to hurry and bring the wood to the kitchen, because he had to go to the synagogue to pray. The dignified donkey driver, with his luxuriant beard and sidelocks, said to him, 'Musai (local name for Jews) also goes to pray?' Rabbi Reuven answered: 'We are Jews and we pray to G-d who gave us his Law from the heavens through Moses our teacher of blessed memory'. 'If you are a Jews', answered the driver, 'explain to me 'In the beginning G-d created the heavens and the earth?' Rabbi Reuven answered, 'Not like he who builds his home on foundations on the earth are the deeds of G-d. He created the heavens before the earth'. The driver

said to him: 'If so, I see that you too are a Jew!' And what is your name?"
asked Rabbi Reuven quickly, for he was afraid of missing the time of
public prayer. 'My name is Israel Khan', said the driver as he went on
his way.

In Kandahar, Mohammed Zai, one of the local notables, has a document
relating his lineage all the way to King Saul.

Every few months a group of traders from the Lewani tribes would
come to Herat. They are tall, dignified and bearded. They had two strings
on their cloaks. They used to bring goods from Pakistan, sell them, and
buy local products to sell in Pakistan. This had been their livelihood from
time immemorial and their main business was with Jews. The leader of
the group had black strings. When asked why he had them and why they
were black, he said that his people were Jews, his mother lit candles on
Sabbath eve and placed them in the corner under a basket, and that they
live as a family among themselves. Since the Temple was destroyed, they
have tied a black string, and will do until the time comes for them to return
to Judaism.'

(Compiled by A. Brin, 1974)

7) Testimony of Mr. Gul, of Jerusalem

The tribes generally live in the area between Kandahar, Ghazni, and
Kabul. They number about four million. Their women light a candle on
Sabbath eve and do not touch the basket where the candle is throughout
the entire Sabbath. They only marry within the tribes. Most of the men
have short sidelocks and the rest of the head is shaved. The following are
some of the tribes: Efratis, Shinwaris, Jajis, Mumandis-Mangali-Menashe,
Musa-Zai, Yusuf-Zai and Yitzhak-Zai (who have special sheep).

They wear a small tallit, wrapping its strings around a button eight
times. There is also the Lewani tribe, which numbers about sixty
thousand; they ride camels and live between Kandahar and Kavita. They
do not drink wine and are very hospitable. One of them always came on
the eve of Yom Kippur to pray, and would stay in the synagogue until the
end of the fast without uttering a sound. He used to retell the tradition of

the Temple and the High Priest on Yom Kippur. Near Mazar Sharif live
a few families who know they are Jewish, but who converted to Islam
because of the price of ritual slaughtering."

8) Testimony of Shalom Dadash, of Jerusalem

When I traveled to Israel, I came by way of Peshawar. On the border
we were stopped for questioning by one of the guards. When he saw that
we were Jews he asked: 'Are we Jews or not, you, see, I wear fringes
(showing his cloak). My father wears fringes, my mother lights candles,
my grandmother lights candles, so are we Jews or not?'

From what he said I learned that he was from the Lewani tribe. He
claims that they are of the tribe of Benjamin (Ben-Amin). I asked him
jokingly: 'Why do you not return to Judaism, and see no need to?'

He answered: 'The day will come when we will return and be Jews!'

As a sign of his esteem he gave us loaves of bread and sent us in honor.
The man was bearded, healthy, and his face looked like a Jewish face. He
looked like those tribesmen who used to come to Herat. Many were
traders, dealing especially with Jews. They liked Jews.

(Compiled by E. Avichail, 1974)

9) Testimony of Mr. Meir Kafi, of Tel Aviv

In the town of Kost near Ghazni there is a duty-free store. I was in it
when a soldier entered who belonged to one of the tribes. He asked for a
silk tablecloth for "Joy Namaz" (place of prayer). 'Why do you buy this?'
I asked him. When he looked at me inquiringly, I told him I was a Jew
and then he said, 'You are like the sun which came out from behind a hill'
and added that all the inhabitants of Kost are cousins of the Jews of the
tribe of Mohammed Zia. I asked 'Do you have written proof of this?' and
he answered: 'You are a Jew, correct? Do not be angry'. 'Why should I
be angry?' I asked, and he continued: 'You know how to write? If so,
show me when you arrived in Afghanistan? We do not have the means to

write, and also we have no books, but you, though you are Jews, have no written (proof) of it'.

I saw members of the Jaji tribe and they had sidelocks, black eyes, and the appearance of Jews. They used to come to Kabul and I asked them why they had sidelocks. They answered that they did not know. They all like the Jews.

I heard from Mr. Rafael Basan of Kabul that the Jews, dressed in Jewish holiday clothes, took a walk through King Zair Khan's Garden in Kabul on the second day of the intermediate days of Passover. The king told them – 'go with the customs of the time, for you are longtime residents here'. In the city of Gur-Sakhar there is a Jewish synagogue, dating before the coming of Mohammed. Because of its archeological importance, the city has an airline link with Kabul.

In the Dar-El-Amman Museum of Kabul there was a black stone that had written on it: "Ana went in G-d's shadow. Betzalel went in G-d's shadow. Fear and trembling will come upon us, and he who is a Jew will be killed, and he who is a Muslim will live. On Wednesday, the 13th of Adar" (the year was not written; it was broken off intentionally, in his opinion).

Someone came from France and related that they had found the stone in Kandahar and 'the year was broken off by the government'. The writing was in Hebrew. He wanted to photograph it but did not find it because it was put inside a storehouse under large stones, and so could not be photographed.

Thirty years ago, the Mohammed Zai tribe said that they were Jews from the tribe of Benjamin, but today they say that they are Aryans.

(Compiled by E. Avichail, 1974)

10) Testimony of Mr. Haim Yitzhak, a leader of the Afghan Community in Tel Aviv

The Afridis light candles, grow sidelocks and do not cook on the Sabbath. When the city of Balkh was rebuilt, some workers came (as work tax) from different cities and among there were many Afridis. They related that they light two candles on Sabbath eve. On the Sabbath they do no cooking. They grow sidelocks and prepare 12 loaves in honor of the Sabbath.

(Compiled by E. Avichail, 1974)

11) Testimony of Mr. Yitshak Dil, of Ra'anana, who immigrated from Afghanistan in 5734/1974

When he was in Kabul he heard of old Torah Scroll pages from Mulmul. He asked to buy them and then heard that there was a complete scroll. He sent a man called Agarjan to buy it but he could not find the man who told of it. (Mr. Kafi heard this testimony, but doubted that there was any basis to the story.)

The French excavated under an old gate at Ghazni (or Kandahar) and found a large stone. It was brought to the museum Dar El Amman in Kabul I saw it and found ancient Hebrew script written on it. I asked the museum director what was written on the stone. He answered that the writing was unknown. I then took out a calendar that I had from Israel, and on it was ancient Hebrew script. I told him it was ancient Hebrew script and he asked me to go to the head director to discuss this. (Mr. Kafi also knows of this fact).

Once I toured with my family in the king's garden in Kabul. The king was there also, and called to us. We approached with fearful honor and kissed his hand as is expected. The king asked me how long the Jews had been in Afghanistan, but I could not answer. He answered that there is a stone according to which the Jews have been there 1,540 years.

(Compiled by E. Avichail, 1974)

12) Testimony of Musa Morduf and Moshe Cohen

Musa Morduf related that he traveled near Herat and Ovah with the governor of the city of Hodja-Tchest. The governor's name was Abdul Rahim Khan. They traveled near the city, where there was a stone in the mountain with Hebrew script (written backwards) on it in plaster. This happened 50 years ago.

Moshe Cohen Ambulo traveled from Kabul to Peshawar. On the way he stayed with the tribesmen. On Sabbath eve a tribesman brought 12 loaves of bread. When asked why, he said that this day was "Akhter", a holiday.

Peshawar has an important (royal) palace and streets named after cities in Israel, including a street called Jerusalem.

I spoke with a member of the Mohammed Zai tribe and asked him what were the signs that they were Jewish. He pointed to his arm and to the place of the phylactery of the head, which they keep shaven.

The Lewani tribe is located near Kandahar, toward the Pakistan border. The people's clothes include something like a tallit with a square piece of cloth (like our tallit). I asked them what it was, but they did not know. They place the garment, which they call Joy-namaz (place of prayer) over their head and shoulders; they use it for prayer.

The police chief of Kabul does not like Jews, but his father did, recognizing the connection of the tribes with the Jews. At the time of the Israeli War of Independence, Muslims came to attack the Jews, and he endangered himself to help defend them. In gratitude we made him a beautiful "Place of Prayer". When we presented him with it, he told us that his family was of the Sons of Israel. When Mohammed came, they had no other religion besides Judaism. He said, "you remained Jews, and we accepted the religion of Mohammed". (Reconstructed testimonies).

(Compiled by E. Avichail, 1974)

13) Testimony of Mr. Yosef Barukh, of Rishon Lezion

Mr. Barukh stayed several days a year in the Pathan villages. He sees a connection to the tribes of Israel, especially with the Afridis, Shinwaris, Jajis and Lewanis – who are like brothers.

They identify themselves with the sons of Israel and they know that they fled from somewhere and came to Afghanistan. Both men and women are tall, have lighter complexions than other local tribes, and many have blue eyes. They are brave warriors and all carry arms (revolvers) with permits.

He saw a woman carrying the haunch of a camel on her shoulder. In another incident he saw a woman give birth in a field, wrap the baby up, and continue to help her husband in his work. They raise animals – sheep and cattle, but there is also agriculture. Those who grow hashish do not use it.

In Balkh there was an important family, friendly with the Barukh family. The sons had Hebrew names, such as Israel, David and Moshe, and most were literate. Some shaved their heads in the middle at the place of the phylacteries. All grew sidelocks and did not touch them, and most had beards.

The Joy-Namaz (Place of Prayer) is used by all the Pathans. Unlike the Muslim rug of prayer it is white, and they keep it very clean. They spread it on the ground for prayers.

Many of the children of the Jaji and other tribes in Balkh wear a type of small tallit under their garment, which is open on both sides and tied together lower down. Asked why they wear it, they told me that it was for protection against enemies and the evil eye.

The children are circumcised at the age of eight days, unlike the Muslims. The ceremony is very joyous, and they slaughter many sheep in celebration.

In Konduz (or Kost) Mr. Barukh saw a wedding ceremony using a canopy, and saw the groom put a ring on the bride's finger.

They do not keep dietary laws, but they do not eat camel meat or horsemeat. They differentiate between clean and unclean birds as do the Jews. They greatly respect "Torat-el-Sharif" – The Law of Moses.

In Mulmul there was a synagogue for the tribes, but it sank into the ground and only the upper section was visible. They do not pray in the direction of Mecca, saying that they do not know exactly where Mecca is, nor in the direction of the Bayt-el-Mukades (Temple).

Women keep family purity and menstruation laws. During menstruation, husbands and wives avoid physical contact. After that they wait seven to nine days and bathe twice at home. Most women go to city bathhouses, if these exist.

The Sabbath is called "Yom-el-Hafta" (seventh day). On Sabbath eve he saw an old woman lighting candles in a cold storage room (used for fruit) in the yard. Asked why she did so, she did not know. Mr. Barukh was told in Balkh of old people who do not cook on the Sabbath. They did not know the reason.

If the brother dies childless, there are levirate marriages in many cases. They keep the law of honoring one's parents in an exemplary fashion. They rise when the father enters, and stand with heads bowed, listening to him obediently. They give alms generously – bags of flour and jugs of oil.

Their spoken language is Afghan (Pashtu). The Jaji are very wealthy. Many live in cities like Kabul and Balkh. He heard in Peshawar that there is a special place of prayer for the Sons of Moses (Musa-Zai). They told him that there is a place behind Peshawar where the sands blow in a storm for six days and stop on the Sabbath. The Sons of Moses are to be found there. When I told him it was certainly the Sambatyon, he did not understand and asked for an explanation.

The Jews fear the tribesmen.

(Compiled by E. Avichail, 1974)

14) Testimony of Mr. Yosef Ben Rahamim, Jewish Agency emissary to Pakistan

He saw the Pathans in Karachi, Pakistan. They are tall and brave. They came to trade and guard. He heard of Jewish customs. They have Mediterranean faces, are honest and trustworthy.

(Compiled by E. Avichail, 1974)

15) Joseph Kessel of France, a well-known author who spent a long time in Afghanistan

The Pushtu tribes have white skin (dark hue) and beautiful faces. Their origin is shrouded in mystery, but they call themselves "Sons of Israel" and they say that their ancestors immigrated to Central Asia from Mesopotamia in the period of Nebuchadnezzar, after the Babylonian exile.[14]

16) Testimony of S. M. Immodin, Professor at Dacca University, Bangladesh

On the Pathans:

This nation was known for its courage and strength. Most scholars, both Eastern and Western, accept the premise that they are of Jewish origin. According to most Eastern historians, the Afghans testify to their being of Jewish origin, though some disagree with this view.

The reason for the change of their names to Afghan names was that the Babylonians and Egyptians persecuted them as Jews, so they fled and began to migrate to escape from the tyrants, and eventually changed their name to Pushton or Pakhton. They were already known by this name in the 6th century C.E.

Some of the proofs of their Jewish origin: During time of plague they sacrifice animals, and smear the doorposts of their homes as in Egypt.

They have a scapegoat to expiate their sins. They keep the custom of Levirate marriages. There are similarities between the Pushtu and Hebrew languages. They celebrate Passover by making unleavened bread. Many have Hebrew names.[15]

17) Testimony of Moshe Khardim, an Amishav emissary and Israeli student who traveled to Afghanistan in the summer of 1975

He heard in Herat from some Jews that the Kakaris, Jajis and Lewanis have clothes with fringes (two at the front). The Shinwaris have a square

---

14   From his book "Afghanistan".
15   Islamic Culture 1949, p. 23 – The Origin of the Afghans.

garment that they spread on the ground to pray on, and the Jews say there are fringes on the garment. All have beards, and the Afridis, Shinwaris, Jajis and Lewanis have sidelocks.

He saw a black stone in a museum with 8-15 lines written in Aramaic and Greek saying: "Respect your father and your elders and do not kill animals" (the stone was from 300 B.C.E.).

In Minerjam in Central Afghanistan there is a stone with the Shield of David on it. There are also pictures of graves with Hebrew writing on them. The graves are about 1,000 years old and have a Hebrew date on them. The Germans photographed these graves and published the photographs in a book. (For instance on one it is written: "Joseph ben Menashe died", in the Persian language with Hebrew script.)

Each tribe has a family tree written on deerskin with gold letters, showing descent from the sons of Jacob until the present head of the tribe. Mr. Khardim heard that the Jajis and the Lewanis converted to Islam because of the threat of death. When he was among the Jajis or Afridis, he found a piece of silver that had the Shield of David on it (this is possibly the silver bracelet which be brought with him and presented to the Amishav organization).

The tribes marry only among themselves. He saw and photographed a beautiful 1,000-2,000-year-old pillar with a Shield of David on it. In Tchastovi there is a school where there is a pillar with a Shield of David (he showed a photograph). Three years ago, one of the Shinwaris came to the synagogue in Kabul and recounted that his grandmother lit candles. He continued coming for six months on Sabbaths and New Moons, and then stopped coming.

A. Scott, in his book "Afghan and Pathan" says that the Abdullis, Saub-Zai and Barukh-Zai belong to the Sons of Israel from the Kingdom of "Gur".[16] He further notes that the Ghilzais, Kurianis, Shinwaris, and Muhamandis are said to belong to the Sons of Israel.[17] The Jajis and Lewanis also live in Kandahar. He did not find amulets among the

16 A. Scott, *Afghan and Pathan*, p. 13.
17 Ibid. p. 18.

children of the Jajis. He heard testimony from one Jew of a tribe that locked their menstruating women in a small room.

Mr. Khardim heard that the king considers himself to be of the tribe of Benjamin. In a book called "the Book of the Covenant" it is written that Jews who did not see the destruction of the First and Second Temple came to the Afghanistan region. Jews of the area relate that they saw fringes and Sabbath candles fifty years ago. They also swear by Moses. The ritual slaughterer, Moshe Naamat, tells that they had a sort of Torah scroll that they would kiss without knowing what it was. The Jews of Afghanistan are not interested in the customs of the Pathans. The Pathans number 16 million: 7 million in Pushtunistan and 9 million in Afghanistan.

Mula Abba, an old doctor in Herat, saw the above-mentioned fringes among the Lewanis. The Jews know they belong to the Ten Tribes, but did not make contact with them because of the location of their dwellings.

The Pathans (Shinwaris?) have "Joy-Namaz" (Place of Prayer) only, but they do not take them off. They resemble Jews. Historians say that the Shinwaris near Jalalabad do not know the Koran and can hardly be considered Muslims. In Nuristan there are "heretics" who accepted Islam only about 50 years ago.

The constant war with Pakistan makes it very dangerous to travel in the border region. All are suspect and the land seems lawless. The economic situation is difficult for lack of modernization. He tried to speak with the tribesmen, but received no response. Most of the tribesmen are shepherds. Vengeance is a popular custom among them. The synagogue in Maimana was built by Jews.

(Reconstructed and taped by A. Bryn and E. Avichail – spring 1975)

18) Testimony of Yaakov Betzalel, of Tel Aviv

The Jewish origin of the tribes is known to the elders and the learned, and is accepted by the people. The tribes: Afridi, Jaji, Shinwari, Rabbani, Lewani, Ashuri (Asher) and others who do not live in the region, were exiled from the land of Israel by Shalmaneser to the Afghanistan region. As written in the Bible, they were exiled to "Hala and Hibur, the Gozan

River and the cities of Medes". In Mr. Betzalel's opinion, Hibur is Peshibur, because "Pesh" in Afghani means fortress. The Gozan River is a large river flowing near Kandahar and emptying into the Indian Ocean near Karachi. On both sides of the river live about 40 million of these people. One of these tribes is the Waziri tribe, meaning "the ministers", and they are considered important people. When Mohammed came, the tribes thought he was the long awaited Messiah and they converted to Islam (on the other hand, the "Benei Israel" in India did not convert to Islam). The Duranis also belong to the Sons of Israel ("Benei Israel"), and according to their tradition they are of the tribe of Benjamin. They came to Afghanistan at the time of the dispute in the desert, according to Rashi, based on the Midrash to the portion Ekev (10:6). Therefore, in the second counting, in the portion Pinchas, only five families appear from the tribe of Benjamin (instead of ten). At the time of the incident of the concubine on the hill, and at the time of the death of Saul and Jonathan at Gilboa, others of the tribe of Benjamin fled and joined their brothers in Afghanistan. The people of Benjamin became rulers, and when the other tribes were exiled and came to Afghanistan they found a Benjaminite regime.

The tribesmen help one another and marry among themselves and not with the Shiites. They love Israel and see the people as cousins: "We converted to Islam and they remained sons of the religion of Moses". The tribes have a tradition of not killing a Jew, even if he is a criminal.

When he was a child of eight, Mr. Betzalel went with his father to a village near Herat to collect a debt. There were Shiite children, who threw stones at them. Suddenly an old man came from the village and chased the children away. He explained to Yaakov Betzalel that the Jews are the Sons of Israel and his tribe is also from the Sons of Israel, and that the Sons of Israel sinned against G-d and are therefore in exile, but his tribe is not in exile.

The Afghanis grow sidelocks on their cheeks and allow the hair above their ears to grow long. When Mr. Betzalel was walking one time with his son after his car broke down between Mazar and Kabul, the tribesmen saw him and attempted to take the child who had sidelocks, thinking that he was from the tribes, until one of them explained that the Jews also grow sidelocks. They swear by Moses and not by Mohammed.

Instead of a large tallit, they wear "Joy-Namaz" (Place of Prayer) on their head and shoulders. The Joy-Namaz has no fringes. An old woman (past menopause) lights Sabbath candles on Friday eve. They place four bricks on four sides of a square and inside place a candle on which they place a ceramic utensil resting on the bricks, to allow oxygen to reach the candle and protect it from the wind.

All the Pathans in Peshawar and the vicinity have Shields of David in their houses. They see them as signs of good luck, and each person acquires one according to his financial ability.

(Compiled by A. Brin, Spring 1975)

19) Testimony of Mr. Levi Dil, of Raanana

The Jaji (Gad), Shinwari (Shimon), Afridi (Ephraim) and Benjamin tribes are all foreign to the region. Mr. Dil thinks that they alone are part of the Jewish people from among the other tribes. The tradition is kept primarily by the elders. According to their tradition, they were exiled by Nebuchadnezzar and came to Pakistan from India. Today they are Muslims. They know of their Jewish origin (Ten Tribes), but they do not know Jewish history.

They look like Jews, and many of them have beards. Some circumcise their sons on the eighth day. A ninety-five year old woman who died recently remembered that she lit candles on the Sabbath.

About two hundred years ago two tribes that identified with their Jewish origin were annihilated in Kandahar, and consequently the other tribes hide their Jewish identity.

In the Museum in Kabul there is a stone that proves their Jewish past, and that they have been in Afghanistan for about fifteen hundred years. Mr. Betzalel visited the museum and saw a very large stone on which was written ancient Hebrew writing. He asked the director about the stone and was told that it had been excavated in Ghazni, and that there was no one who could read it, until someone was brought from Paris for this purpose.

He spoke with a man from the tribe who told him about a dynasty seventy generations old that proves its Jewish origin.

Mr. Dil believes that the tribes are dispersed only between Iraq and India.

(Compiled by A. Brin, Spring 1975)

20) Testimony of Shalom Siman-Tov, of Ramat Shikma

He knows the Afridi, Jaji, Shinwari and Lewani tribes. The Hebrew names Ephraim, Gad, Shimon and Levi are known amongst them. The Pushtu language is similar to Hebrew. The tribes number seven million and live in the border region. They look like Jews. They keep their sidelocks very meticulously. They are strong, with beautiful eyes, and wear a four-cornered garment without fringes, called "Kafan". There are Hebrew names among them. Some women light candles in honor of the Sabbath.

Once Mr. Siman-Tov had to remain among the tribes on the Sabbath because of business (perhaps this was among the Shinwari). He saw an old woman lighting an oil lamp in the middle of the room on Sabbath eve (similar to the oil lamps of the Jews). Afterwards she spread a mat over it. When she was asked why, she said that it was a remembrance from the time when they were Jews. Three signs remained of their Jewishness: fringes, sidelocks and the Sabbath candles. Mr. Siman-Tov asked the old woman why they converted to Islam, and she answered that it was because they were killed and tormented, and since they heard that the Muslims said "Allah" ("G-d" in Arabic) they agreed to convert to Islam. Consequently they do not wish to reveal their Judaism. Furthermore, she claimed: "We are the real Jews, not you".

When the State of Israel was established, Mr. Siman-Tov heard that many from among the tribes wanted to immigrate to Jerusalem to help their Jewish brothers, but when they revealed their purpose the authorities did not allow them to go there.

The king, who was expelled, liked the Jews, with whom he lived when he was studying in France. The Afghan tribes are nomadic shepherds, and very hospitable. It is not dangerous to stay among them.

(Compiled by A. Brin, Spring 1975)

21) Testimony of Baruch Mula, of Bnei Brak

"I became acquainted with the tribes when they visited Herat on business, and also when I stayed for a certain period in Kabul and Kandahar".

He had heard of the Jaji-Gad, Shinwari-Shimon, Afridi-Ephraim and Lewani-Levi tribes, since the tradition of their origin is well-known in Afghanistan. He saw people of the Lewani tribe who wore garments open at the side and at the bottom, similar to a four-cornered garment, with one string in each corner. He heard from the tribesmen that their old women light a candle on Sabbath eve and cover it with a big basket.

The royal family said that it was of the lineage of the tribe of Benjamin. The kings are known for their friendliness towards the Jews. Once the king Habibullah Khan ordered food from the Jews in order to demonstrate his friendly attitude towards them. The family tree of the Afghan kings is mentioned in their memoirs.

The administrator of the city of Maimana is reputed to have told the Jews who came to visit him, "I am a Jew and you are not", and when they mentioned the name of Moses our teacher to him he stood in memory of him. He once sent his soldiers on a Sabbath to bring vinegar from the Jews, and because it was the Sabbath a fight broke out and his soldiers were assaulted. When thy returned and told the administrator that the Jews refused to provide vinegar because it was the Sabbath, he remembered and said, "If so, better that you would have been killed". To this day many of the tribesmen are bandits, but they distribute the booty among the poor. They are physically very strong, and when they fought the British they also sent their women into battle. They are independent. They trust the Jews in matters of commerce, even though the Jews trade in forbidden merchandise.

They would tell the Jews: "We are Jews and you are not". Once my friend asked them, "how do you know you are Jew?" They said they had a sign and pointed to their sidelocks. They are friends of Israel.

(Compiled by A. Brin, 1975)

22) Testimony of Menashe Rabani, supported by Shimshon Kashi, who immigrated to Israel from Kabul in 1974

He recounted that all the Afghan tribes have a tradition that they once belonged to the Jewish people. He knows the famous tribes – Afridi, Jaji, Shinwari, Lewani (Waziri) by their Hebrew names, and sees their names only as an Afghan translation. The tribes differ from other tribes in the area by their external appearance. The Jajis are tall, light complexioned and green-eyed. They do not marry with other tribes.

Once he traveled with a friend to the area of the Afghan tribes, and spent the night there. He was sent to the sheikh's house. There a feast consisting of various dishes and mutton was served on wide trays. The two feared that they would be asked to eat non-kosher food, but the sheikh asked to bring them eggs and to cook them in a separate utensil used for making tea, and also to bring yogurt. After the meal, the shieikh said that the guests are from the Sons of Abraham, Isaac and Jacob, and they themselves are also sons of Jacob, but they converted to Islam in the past. However, they keep a parchment scroll on which is written of their origin from the tribes of Israel. At the end of days the Mahdi (Messiah in Persian) will come and guide them back to Israel. According to Mr. Rabani, other tribal heads have similar scrolls.

He also relates that when he was a young man he was riding in a truck in the city of Mazar, and beside him sat a gentile soldier who punched him until he started to cry. People asked why he was crying, and he showed them the marks from the blows that he had received from the soldier. Then, their officer stood up and reprimanded the soldier, and said to him: "Ask your father and your elders and they will tell you that once we were also Jews but we were not steadfast".

At their weddings the tribesmen sing a lot about Moses. There was a Jewish community at Mulmul until a hundred and thirty years ago, but they converted to Islam. To this day, they keep their Torah scrolls in a locked place, and anyone who has a request comes there and touches the lock. Many of them have Hebrew names like Samuel, Simeon etc.

They grow sidelocks to the middle of their cheeks, but the custom is not observed strictly. The women light candles on the Sabbath and cover them with baskets. As a remembrance of fringes they wear a garment three to four meters long, and they fold it on their necks like a scarf. They also tie a string at the bottom of their garments even if it is not separated into corners. The tradition is not observed by the young, but the attitude towards the Jews is good.

(Compiled by A. Brin, 1975)

23) Testimony of Abba M., of Bnei Brak

In his opinion a distinction must be made between the Persian-speaking tribes (Tajiki) and the Afghan speaking tribes (Pushtu?). The first group includes the royal family, the Mohamadanis and others. The second group includes the Sardis, Kandaharis, Ghilzais, Lewanis, Jajis and others (he does not remember well). The Yusuf Zai families are the aristocrats among them. Three tribes belong to the Sons of Israel – Afridis, Shinwaris and Waziris. They live together in the border region around Kabul-Peshawar-Kavita-Kandahar, in long tent-camps. The tribes that he visited were very wild and illiterate. They carried out mathematical calculations using a marked rope. They have flocks of sheep but also live by stealing from strangers. A stranger is liable to be killed by them. They consider the man who kills and steals the most to be a hero. They launch attacks also on Indians, pillaging and kidnapping the daughters and converting them to Islam. It is accepted to marry up to seven wives.

Discipline is firmly administered by the tribal chief in all matters. They are very rich and completely independent. The Afghan government fears them. Each tribe sees itself as the strongest and they do not intermarry even with the other tribes. They are not aware of world events, but, conversely, when one becomes friendly with them, they are extremely hospitable.

"Once I met Mohammed Khan Tarazi, the head of a large Afridi tribe. After an extended stay with him, I told him I was Jewish. He had difficulty understanding what a Jew was, but after he understood, he said that they came to these areas with the Nebuchadnezzar exile from Israel, and that they were also Jews. After the coming of Mohammed they converted to Islam. I told them that they should be proud of their past. I asked them why they retained no customs showing their Judaism. The head of the tribe answered that they still kept three customs: they have a large four-cornered garment (without fringes) that they wear on their head and shoulders; they are careful not to shave their sidelocks (they shave their heads and beards, but not the parts of the sidelocks beside the ears). Afterwards he took me to his tent, and his wife showed me the third custom – an oil lamp that they lit every Friday afternoon. They cover the lamp with a very large basket so that it will not be extinguished. (A lamp like this is also found among Afghan Jews). They say that this custom of lighting the lamp is slowly being forgotten, and they see the lamp as a sign of their Jewishness. They consider that it will bring them good luck if the candle does not go out until the end of the Sabbath.

Later, his wife took me to the corner of the tent and took out a small package that was very well hidden, and she bowed down before it. When I asked her about it, she said that when someone is sick in the village, they place the package under their head and they will get well immediately. When I wished to open the package she said, "If you cpen it you will die". They told me that there are other such packages all over the region. I asked that they show me other packages, and they brought me to an old woman over 100 years old, known as a healer of the sick. She also did not allow me to open the package and said 'a pity that you should die young.' I pleaded with them and stayed the night, until finally she agreed to opening of the package, but not in her presence. I opened it and found a small book of Psalms written in Hebrew but which was difficult to read, and also a picture of a menorah of the type that decorates Sephardic synagogues. When I asked her how she heals sick people, she told me that she knows a couple of names of angels, among which I identified the name Mikhi (Michael?). She told me that she received the package and the secret of the names of the angels from her mother. Naturally she refused to give me the package.

They circumcise on the eighth day when they have money for it. They do not know Muslim customs well."

(Compiled by A. Brin, 1975)

24) Testimony of Zion Solomon, who immigrated from Karachi in 1949

The tribal members who live in Pakistan sometimes leave the tribal framework and go to the city where they work in various occupations. This was the case in Karachi.

A Rabbani waiter in Karachi with whom Mr. Solomon came into contact and who saw that Mr. Solomon acted like Jews, said that they are also from the Sons of Israel exiled from Babylon. As proof, he said that he circumcised his son at the age of eight days. He does not eat meat unless it has been ritually slaughtered, and not by the breaking of the neck as in the manner of the Indians. They know the day of rest is the seventh day and they light the candles on the eve of the Sabbath. He had an amulet around his neck as did the other Pathans, and as do all the Muslims, but whereas the Muslims have amulets with verses from the Koran, sometimes written also externally, the Pathan amulets have nothing on the outside, and "Shema Yisrael" is sometimes written on the inside.

(Compiled by A. Brin, 1975)

25) Testimony of Mr. Hananel Merziof of Tel Aviv, who lived in Peshawar – Pakistan from 1935 to 1948

In 1942 there was a Jewish chaplain from the British army who went to visit the Shinwari tribe. He met the head of the tribe, Nabob Huti, in his home. Nabob Huti is the father of Nabob Mordan who was in close contact with the Merziof family. The head of the tribe told the Jewish chaplain about the book of his family's origin, that he wanted it translated into English and published, but Muslim zealots had burnt it. Notwithstanding, he had in his possession an original copy.

The chaplain had heard that President Y. Ben-Zvi had sent an American to Peshawar in order to obtain a book of genealogy, but was unsuccessful in his endeavor.

Nabob Huti related that Nebuchadnezzar had brought them because of their bravery to the mountain region of Afghanistan-Pakistan. They had accepted Islam because of its similarity to the Law of Israel.

The head of the tribe said: 'Our blood is Jewish blood; we dress differently from the other tribes. We have a garment, different by its white color, and the fact that it is hand-woven. We wear a skullcap and a Joy-namaz (as do all) over our heads.' The Pathans have small sidelocks and usually have beards. The Pathans are pleasant people and brave. Their faces are Semitic and some have light blue eyes.

They know that about 500 years ago they had a Torah scroll, but they could not read it. When the king of Iran came to visit them, he asked who they were, and they said that they did not exactly know, but that they had a book, according to which they know their identity. With the king was a Jewish minister who discovered that the book was a Torah scroll, and he told them that they were Jews.

On Friday, old women light a candle in the evening, but do not know why. The chaplain saw the candle in the room and asked about it. He was told that lighting "was an ancient tradition". They number some three to four million.

The chaplain heard that there was a nabob (prince) who said that they have to fight with the British against the Germans to protect the Jewish people. They do not eat horse and camel meat.

The English Jewish chaplain asked about family purity, and was told that they immerse in a river and do not touch their spouses for three days. They marry only within the tribe.

In Landi Kotal (the mountain country) Mr. Merziof visited the Jaji, Shinwari and Afridi tribes. They are drivers and deal in transport. They know English and so it is possible to meet and speak with them in Peshawar. They have radios and the place is accessible by road and not dangerous because they are very hospitable. The rich have houses and the poor live in tents. There are shepherds and farmers and also merchants. They are wise and brave. They sell hashish and also smoke it. They respect their mothers very much. When a child is born they give him a rifle.

(Compiled by E. Avichail)

26) Testimony of Mr. Pinchas Yekutieli, of Jerusalem

I heard that the kings of Afghanistan have a book of genealogy. This I heard from members of the royal family. I saw fringes, but only at the front, where they have two strings on their clothes.

Some wear sidelocks and some do not. Every community and tribe has a special garment. Every tribe has a chief. Some tribes have a proven link to Israel through their names, such as Suleiman Khil and Musa Zai. They live on the Pakistani border. Some of them know they were Jews, but most do not believe this, and are already assimilated.

(Compiled by E. Avichail)

27) Abba Gul of Jerusalem

I heard that the Afghanis have signs that they were once Jews. For example, they light candles on Sabbath eve and cover them with a basket. Royalty is of the tribe of Benjamin.

28) Mr. Moshe Naamat, former head of the Jewish community in Herat, a ritual slaughterer and circumciser. He immigrated to Israel in 1978.

Each Afghan family has a book of genealogy, according to which they belong to the people of Israel; they keep the book hidden. He knows the names of the tribes: Jaji, Afridi, Shinwari, Jamshivi (Menashe).

They strictly observe the laws of impurity and purity pertaining to a menstruating woman. One of the laws observed is that the woman is isolated for 15 days.

They keep the "Joy Namaz" always with them, even when they are not wearing it, and they keep it clean.

On Sabbath eve they light a kerosene lamp, and put it under a basket until the end of the Sabbath.

They have first names not found among the Muslims, such as Israel and Jacob.

Mr. Naamat has brochures in German in which is written that German researchers found 11th and 12th century graves in Chaghcharan with inscriptions in Persian script and in the Hebrew language.

(Compiled by E. Avichail)

THE KASHMIRI NATION
IN NORTHERN INDIA

The Inhabitants of Kashmir

The State of Kashmir in Northern India borders Pakistan and Afghanistan to the east and consists of a very wide valley surrounded by high mountains. Its inhabitants number 5-7 million and are different from the other inhabitants of India. Generally, they have lighter complexions and a Semitic appearance. Today, most are Muslims.

An interesting tradition passed down among the inhabitants of Kashmir regards their ancestry from the Ten Tribes.[1] This tradition is supported by extensive literature, written both by the people of Kashmir and by others. Notably, the people of Kashmir, even though they are Muslims, are sympathetic towards Israel and the Jews. Their interest in their origin has also led to interest in the Jewish people.

There is apparent willingness among the people of Kashmir to learn about Judaism, and perhaps also to return to their roots – to the Jewish people. In 1982, a national committee of professors from Kashmir requested permission to visit Israel in order to research their origins. Unfortunately, due to lack of funding, the committee did not make the trip.

Like the history of most peoples in the region, the history of the Kashmiri nation is shrouded in mystery.

The History

Many Kashmir researchers believe that most of the inhabitants of Kashmir are descendants of the Ten Tribes, who were exiled in 722 B.C.E. and wandered along the Silk Route through the countries of the

---

[1] See *Encyclopedia Judaica*: Kashmir.

East, Persia and Afghanistan, until they reached and settled in the Kashmir Valley. Others believe the wanderings began approximately 300 years later. It is generally agreed among researchers that the wanderers settled in the Kashmir Valley and kept their traditions until they were forcibly converted to Islam.

Traditions

In Yusmarg (Handwara), on the border of Pakistan, there is one group that calls itself to this day "Bnei Israel". However, many inhabitants of Kashmir believe this ancient name relates to all Kashmiris.

Some people of Kashmir believe that Jesus Christ did not die on the Cross, but arrived in his search for the Ten Tribes to the Kashmir Valley, where he lived until his death.[2] They even point out his grave in Kashmir.

An even stranger tradition belongs to a small community near the Wular Lake, which points to the grave of Moses and calls places in the area Bnei Peor, Pisgah, Heshbon and Mount Nebo (place names found in the Bible).

According to another tradition, King Solomon came to the Kashmir Valley and, thanks to his great wisdom, helped the inhabitants by regulating the flow of the Jalum River. This tradition is also connected to the place "Takht-I-Suleiman" meaning Solomon's Throne, located above Srinagar, the capital of Kashmir.

Literature

The two primary historians of Kashmir, Mulla Nadiri[3] and Mulla Ahmad,[4] establish, without a trace of doubt, that the people of Kashmir are descended from the Jews.[5]

---

2   A. Faber-Kaiser, *Jesus Died in Kashmir*, Scribner 1977.
3   Mulla Nadiri: *Tarikh-iKashmir* (The History of Kashmir), 1413, Persian.
4   Mulla Ahmad, *Waqqya-I-Kashmir* (The Events of Kashmir), 1899.
5   A. Faber-Kaiser, *Ibid.*

Abdul Qadir bin Qaziul-Quzat Wazil Ali Khan is of the same opinion.[6]

The priest Kataro, in his book, "The General History of the Moghul Empire" wrote that the Kashmir people are the descendants of the Israelites.[7]

The traveling Arab historian El Biruni wrote, in the 12th century, in a report on India: "In the past only Jews were allowed to enter Kashmir". The priest Monserrate said, in the time of Vasco de Gama, in the fifteenth century: "All the inhabitants of this area who have been living here since ancient times can trace their ancestry, according to their race and their customs, to the Jews; their features, their general physical appearance and clothing, and their ways of conducting business, all show that they are similar to the Jews in Europe."[8]

Books which discuss this subject today are "Jesus Died in Kashmir" by A. Faber-Kaiser and "Hindu Kashmir" by Professor F.M. Hassanen, the director of the national museum.

Dr. Aziz Ahmad Kurshi concurs with the above opinion in his book "Asrar-I-Kashmir" (The Mystery of Kashmir), published in both Urdu and English, and the same idea has been stated in numerous other books.

Mr. Ikbal Chapri, the owner of a houseboat named "Haifa" in Srinagar, has written about this topic in the Srinagar newspapers.

The following lists of names is compiled from the philological evidence about tribal and place names in Kashmir literature, and compared with Hebrew.

6   Abdul Qadir bin Qaziul-Quzat Wazil Ali Khan, Hashmat-i-Kashmir.
7   A. Faber-Kaiser, *Ibid.*
8   W. J. Fischel, *Yehudim Veyahadut Bemishpat Hamoguli* (Jews and Judaism in Mogul Law).

Names of Tribes and Groups in Kashmir

Abri – Ibri	Matri – Matri	Zaru – Zera
Amal – Amal	Moza – Moza	Gaddi – Gaddi
Asheriya – Asher	Musa – Moses	Gadha – Gad
Attai – Ittai	Nehru – Naor	Gareb – Gareb
Azri – Azriel	Sahul – Saul	Jomer – Gomer
Bal – Baal	Shuah – Shuah	Haqqaq – Hukok
Baniyah – Beniyah	Suleimani – Solomon	Shai – Ishai
Berot – Beeroth	Tamar – Tamar	Israel – Israel
Bilgai – Bilgah	Tellah – Telah	Kahana – Cohen
Caleb – Caleb	Tiku – Tekoa	Kalkul – Kalkul
Dand – Dan	Tola – Tola	Kanaz – Kenaz
Gabba – Gaba	Zadu – Zadok	Lavi – Levi
Mallak – Melech (= king)	Zartan – Zaretan	

Names of Places in Kashmir

Ach-Bal (Anantnag) – Ashbel

Amoni (Kulgam) – Amon

Amariah (Srinagar) – Amariah

Aner-wan (Srinagar) – Aner

Ara-Ham (Anantnag) – Ara

Ara-Guttu (Kulgam) – Ara

Ara-bal (Kulgam) – Arah

Ara-Mullat (Kulgam) – Ara

Aror (Awantipur) – Aroer

Astor (Kulgam) – Ashtaroth

Bahan (Kulgam) – Bohan

Balpura (Awantipur) – Baalpeor

Bani-Ruth (Kulgam) – Ruth

Barzilla (Kulgam and Srinagar) – Barzillai

Ben-hara – Ham

Behatpoor (Handwara) – Bethpeor

Dan-sok (Kulgam) – Dan

Doru (Anantnag and Gilgit) – Dor

Gochan (Anantnag) – Goshen

Hara-mog (Anantnag) – Hara

Heshba (Handwara) – Heshbon

Kahan (Awantipur) – Kahan

Kalkol (Kulgam) – Kalkul

Keran (Kernah) – Cheran

Lasharoun (Srinagar) – Lasharon

Lavi-pura (Handwara) – Levi

Lyddan (Palwana) – Lod

Mamre (Srinagar) – Mamre

Mattan (Anantnag) – Mattan

Median-pura (Kulgar) – Midian

Nabudaal (Handwara) – Mt. Nebo

Nine-Wa (Anantnag) – Nineveh

Perah (Udampur) – Para

Phallu (Kulgam) – Phallu

Pishgah (Handwara) – Pisgah

Rissi-Pura (Awantipur) – Rissah

Shipoan (Kulgam) – Shopan

Sukait – Succoth

Suru (Bhawan) – Shur

Takht-I-Sulaiman (Srinagar) – Solomon

Tarelu (Awantipur) – Taralah (Judah)

Teman-kot (Handwara) – Taman

Uri – Uri

Tema-pura (Kulgam) – Tema

Bushan (Pamir) – Bashan

Dottan (Balistan) – Dothan

Gilgit – Gilgal

Gozana – Gozan

Jehial (Gilgit) – Yechiel

Kirjuth (Ladakh) – Kiryath

Lhasa (Tibet) – Lasha/Laish

Moserah (Kenskar) – Moseroth

Pishon (Zenskar) – Pison

Rabath (Pamir) – Rabbah

Rezin (Zanskar) – Rezin (Nechemia)

Samaryah (Zanska) – Samaria

In addition, the name "Joo" (Jew?) appears as a suffix to many names in Kashmir. The name Israel is also fairly common, as among the Pathans. This name is not used at all by Muslims.

The Kashmiris practice a number of Jewish customs that have not been sufficiently studied. These include lighting a candle for the Sabbath, growing side-locks and a beard, displaying the *Magen David*, and others.

Kashmiris adjust the lunar calendar to the summer calendar, in order to celebrate a Spring festival called "Pasca" (the Hebrew word *"Pascha"* means Passover).

Educated members of the Kashmiri tribes have expressed their wish to return to the Jewish people.

THE KAREN PEOPLE OF MYANMAR (BURMA) AND THAILAND[9]

The Karen number today about 5-7 million. They are Mongolian in appearance. According to their tradition, they came to Myanmar from the Chinese state Yunan.

Until the appearance of the missionaries in the early nineteenth century, the Karen had no writing or literature and their entire tradition was passed down orally.

The Karen people are known to be pleasant, humble, hospitable, industrious and loyal. They are great lovers of music, sing well, and are familiar with Western music.

They, like others who trace their origins to the Ten Tribes, are fighting for their independence. Their country is in the southern part of Myanmar (formerly Burma), and they hope to gain complete independence in their region. They are preparing themselves for self-rule.

The belief in "Y'wa"

A remarkable thing in Karen history is the "Y'wa" tradition, a clear connection to the Hebrew tradition and the Hebrew name "Y-H-W-H" in the Bible. Clearly at one time they had real contact with the Bible and its stories.

They have stories of the creation of the world, the removal of mankind from the world by the flood during the time of Noah, and the scattering of mankind at Babel.

---

9   From the book: "A Look at Burmese History" – V. S. Desai, and other sources.

The Lost Scroll

The Karen maintain a firm belief that they once possessed a "book" (scroll) that contained the law of "Y'wa" and basic tenets of their true faith.

They believe their book was lost because the elders did not observe the faith and commandments in it.

They have a prophetic tradition that their "lost scroll" will be found and returned by the "white brother".

Songs about the Lost Scroll:

Our golden book that "Y'wa" gave
Our silver book that he gave
The elders did not keep
It was lost and wandered to strangers

The principles of belief in G-d in the following Karen song are very similar to those in Jewish tradition:

"Y'wa" is eternal, he existed alone
Before any creature was created
His kingdom stands forever
And he is G-d forever
Two worlds will pass and he exists.
He is perfect in all
From generation to generation his glory shines
"Y'wa", without change – forever
He was the beginning of the creation
And he has no end
He is the beginning of the world
"Y'wa"'s life is eternal
All the worlds will not imagine him
Perfect in all perfection
And he will not be absent ever.

Sacrifices

The Karen people, like the ancient Israelites, offer sacrifices. Their prayers indicate belief that their sacrifices – bulls, cows and goats – are required as atonement for sins and to ensure that the land will yield produce.

Conversion to Christianity

When the great American missionary Adoniram Judson arrived in Burma in 1813, he came to a Karen village and showed them the Bible, confirming to them that their "lost book" had been found. Many Karen who knew the prophecy of the lost book became Baptists. One Karen obtained a copy of the Bible and brought it to his village. Men, women and children came to kiss and stroke the Bible with wonder, tears and thanksgiving. They decided never to be separated from it again. Christianity spread more rapidly among the Karen than among any other people in Burma.

The proselytes quickly became the social elite of the Karen.

Because the customs and traditions of the Karen are similar to those of their "relatives," the Shinlung in India and Burma, it is possible that these two peoples (and perhaps also the Shan) have a shared history in Szechwan in western China, where the Chiang tribe, to be discussed below, lives.

Amishav contact with the Karen

In 1996, the author and Micha Gross visited Burma and met Karen people, Christian scholars and religious leaders. A (Christian) bishop told the author that the Karen people are aware of their Israelite origins and that it was a mistake to believe that their 'lost book' was the Christian New Testament presented them by missionaries.

In 1998 the author, together with Micha Gross and Hillel Halkin, visited Karen people in Thailand with the objective of learning what had been written in the Karen's 'lost book'. The author met with people in isolated jungle villages who had never been in contact with Christianity or the Bible, yet could recall stories they believed to be from their 'lost book' about Adam and Eve, the Garden of Eden, the Flood and the Tower of Babel.

Today, Amishav is in contact with a group of Karen interested in returning to Judaism and the Jewish people. The group is attempting to translate the author's book Judaism into their language. One young Karen woman came to Israel some years ago and completed orthodox conversion.

THE SHINLUNG TRIBE (MENASHE) ON THE INDIA-MYANMAR BORDER

Background

The Shinlung Tribe, numbering between one and two million, lives in the mountainous region which straddles the border between India and Myanmar (formerly Burma). On the Myanmar side, a few hundred thousand live in the Chin Mountains, principally in the Tidim area. Nearly a million Shinlung live on the Indian side, in the states of Mizoram and Manipur. Mizoram is inhabited solely by Shinlung, whose principal language is Mizo. They have autonomy subordinate to the Indian government.

The prevalent languages among the Shinlung in Manipur are Manipuri and Kuki. Among the clans (large families), there are about 50 different dialects (for example, Gangata, Wipa and Hamar). Sometimes this makes communication difficult. Most Shinlung in Manipur also know Mizo.

The tradition of their exile

After the conquest of the Ten Tribes by Assyria in the year 722 BCE, the Tribes were taken by Shalmaneser to Assyria, and then sent to Halah, Habor and the Gozan River. By 457 BCE, the Tribe of Menashe had settled in Persia, where it remained during the rule of Darius and Ahasuerus.

Following the conquest of Persia, Afghanistan and India by Alexander the Great in 331 BCE, the Tribes were exiled to Afghanistan (Pakhton) and other countries, where they became shepherds and fell into idolatry.

With the Islamic conquest, they were forced to convert to Islam. Because they spoke Hebrew, they were called the "Semitic Speakers".

Throughout this entire period, they are said to have possessed a Torah scroll that was guarded by the elders and priests.

Continuation of their wanderings

From Afghanistan, the wanderers continued eastward, via Hindu Kush, and reached Tibet and the Chinese border. From there, they followed the Wei River until they reached central China.

A settlement was established in Kaifeng in the year 231 CE. The Chinese treated them cruelly and forced them into slavery; thus began a process of assimilation. In reaction to these pressures, a part of the people fled to caves in the mountain region, where they acquired the names "Cave People" and "People of the Mountains". They lived in terrible poverty for approximately two generations. During that period, they still had the Torah scroll with them.

When they were expelled from the cave area, the Torah scroll was lost, or perhaps stolen and burned by the Chinese. The priests continued to hand down traditions orally, including ritual observances of worship, until the early nineteenth century.

From the Valley of the Caves, known as "Kawil" or "Shin Lung," they migrated westward, passing through Thailand (Siam), the Kila Valley and the Kendi Mountains until reaching Lantchuan and Shan. From there they journeyed to Burma. In Burma, they wandered along the river until they reached Mandalai. From there, they continued to Kalmiyo in the Chin Mountains. In the eighteenth century, some migrated to the Manipur and Mizoram area where they were considered refugees from China.

Traditions and history

A clear tradition of Shinlung history was transmitted orally from generation to generation, primarily by songs and stories. No literature remains. If any literature did exist, the missionaries worked to destroy it. Nonetheless, a clear tradition of a relationship to Zion and the Land of Israel remains. At the center of this tradition is the knowledge that they are descendants of the Tribes of Manasseh and Ephraim, who came from the Land of Israel to the West, through Afghanistan, the Himalayas, Mongolia, Tibet, China, Thailand and Burma to India, where they have lived for many years, principally in the states of Mizoram and Manipur.

One of their common names is "Lu-Si" which means "the Ten Tribes". Like the Karen people, the Shinlung are familiar with stories of the Bible even though they had no encounter with Christianity or Judaism before the arrival of Christian missionaries. Like the Karen, upon the arrival of Christian missionary Adoniram Judson in 1813 with copies of the Bible (including the New Testament), the Shinlung became very excited and willing to convert to Christianity.

The Shinlung believe, as do the Keren people, in one G-d called "Y'wa" and they call out this name when offering sacrifices. The name may be pronounced only at the time of the sacrifice and when making a serious oath. They are not allowed to write the name (and for this reason some even mispronounce the name as "Z'wa").

They, too, have a tradition that the Chinese stole the holy scroll in their possession prior to their flight from China southwards ("it was eaten by dogs"). They regard the Karen people as their kin.

Relationship to the Tribes of Manasseh and Ephraim

As noted, they have a tradition of relationship to the tribe of Manasseh. Only recently it emerged that they also have a very strong connection to the tribe of Ephraim.

The names **Manasseh, Menassiya or Menassiya-Pa** (Father Menashe) and others are an important part of their existence. When performing a commandment they mention their identity as the Tribe of Manasseh so they will not be harmed. When approaching a strange village, and in some prayers, they announce, "The Sons of Manasseh are coming".

When **Male Chala**, one of their leaders, announced some fifty years ago that he had seen a vision, according to which the time had come to immigrate to the land of their forefathers, to Israel, this was quite obvious and logical in their eyes and they awaited a redemption that did not come.

They sought assistance, to no avail, from world Jewish leaders. Around 1970 Tribal leaders decided to return to Judaism before returning to Zion. They sought Jewish sources, studied and observed commandments. They circumcised themselves and their families. They built synagogues, in which they prayed in Hebrew from prayer books that they translated and printed. They observed the Sabbath and holidays to the best of their ability. They sent their youth to study at the ORT school in Bombay (with separate classes for boys and girls), at a distance of some one thousand kilometers from their homes on the Myanmar border.

The author first learned of the Shinlung in 1979, some seven years after they had begun to live as Jews. After about two years' correspondence, they were asked to send two youth to Israel. In 1980, Gideon Rey and Shimon Isak (Jin) arrived in Israel, where they lived three years at a kibbutz *ulpan* and studied one year in a yeshiva. The history of the Shinlung was documented in material they submitted to Amishav.

Also in 1980, the author received a letter from an important personality in Mizoram, India, concerning a dispute among the Shinlung about their being descendants of Ephraim and Manasseh (sons of Joseph). The same question also arrived through the Israeli Embassy in India: **"Who is more important according to Judaism, Ephraim or Manasseh?"** This was the first time the author had heard of people who consider themselves descendants of Ephraim.

During and subsequent to the author's trip to Mizoram in 1997, more information was gathered about this group among the Shinlung called 'Ephraim'. In 1998, Mr. Sailo, a scholar who runs their history institute, maintained that they number about 2,250,000 out of the total of over 4 million Shinlung. Naturally, the veracity of the Shinlung claim to Manasseh (son of Joseph) and the Ten Tribes is reinforced by the existence of this second group of Shinlung who claim descent from Ephraim – Joseph's other son.

Ancient Shinlung Customs (some still in practice)

The Priests

In every village there lived a priest (related to the High Priest Aaron), whose priesthood was was passed on by inheritance. He was responsible for the spiritual and other needs of the village, together with the village chief. In large villages, there were two priests. The priests were thought to have superior powers. They engaged in worship, care of the sick, assisting in cases of hardship and, primarily, in offering sacrifices.

The Priest's Clothing

The priest wore a white tunic. On his chest he wore a kind of breastplate woven from bamboo leaves, and blue fringes hung from his belt. On the breastplate there were two pockets in which were two black polished stones. The breastplate was fastened at the bottom to an embroidered blue sash. There was also an embroidered coat. On his head was a kind of crown. Only an important priest was dressed this way.

The Priest's Duties

In case of illness, the priest was called to bless the sick person and offer a sacrifice for his recovery, and to placate the forces of evil. The priest would slaughter a goat or chicken and smear its blood on the ear, back and legs of the sick person, while reciting verses from the Torah (Leviticus 8:24; 14:14). If several people in the same family were ill, he also sprinkled blood from the sacrifice on the lintel and the two doorposts at the entrance to the house.

The same type of sacrifice was performed in times of community distress, such as plagues, earthquakes or storms, and for the general welfare of the village. If a pig was sacrificed, the priest did not eat it. When a sacrifice was made for a sick person, they tied strings in the form of a Star of David over the altar. For a sick person, the sacrifice was sometimes offered on the balcony of the sick person's home. For the village, the sacrifice was offered in a courtyard or on a neighboring hill.

In the Chin Mountains in Myanmar, there is a special dais for sacrifices in almost every home. The sacrifice is eaten by the household, the priest and invited guests.

Sacrifices of atonement and thanksgiving

The sacrifices called "Noy Pi" were intended for "Y'wa" (whose name could be uttered only during the sacrifice or when making a serious oath) and offered on a four-cornered altar of rough stones.

Important sacrifices, on holidays, were offered on a hilltop (like the Chiang, in China). The sacrifice was made after sunset. They sprinkled the blood on the four corners of the altar. The innards were burned and the meat eaten by the people and the priests. It was obligatory to eat the sacrifice during the night; if not, it had to be buried. They ate the meat without breaking bones. One type of sacrifice ("Sah-Sir") was completely burnt. They used to eat sacrifices of white hens.

It seems there was a special sacrifice for Passover called "halankal," which means 'to pass over'. They ate this sacrifice, also, without breaking bones.

The Shinlung had a box in which there was a structure in the form of the temple, placed next to the altar (they did not worship it). Beside the box was placed a black stone sprinkled with blood (like the Chiang). This stone has a special value, both for hunting and for healing. (It is unclear whether these customs are still practiced.)

Calendar

The Shinlung use a lunar calendar, like the Jewish/Hebrew calendar.

Prohibition on eating blood

Ancient Shinlung practice prohibits eating blood. They do not eat animals without first draining the blood.

Leprosy

The priest had an important role in the case of leprosy. He identified the leprosy and sent the leper to live outside the village (in the jungle). The leper's family helped him from the border of the camp, if necessary. After recovery, he returned to the camp and immersed himself. The priest sacrificed a bird in the field for him – the wings were burned and the feathers scattered to the wind. (It is unclear whether this is still practiced.)

Marriage

There is no marriage without a priest. The priest asks the bride and groom if they are prepared to live together with unlimited devotion, even in times of illness and disability. Gifts are exchanged between the couple. The priest chants next to the altar. Both return to their homes during that day; after nightfall, the bride is escorted to the groom's home.

Circumcision

According to an ancient tradition, on the eighth day after the birth of a male, a ritual called "zangboi" was performed. As a relative pulled back the foreskin, the priest used two sharp heated flints to sever the foreskin and circumcise the baby. The father or the grandfather then announced the baby's name. Before the circumcision, while the priest chanted, the mother and child passed near a large flame.

Even today, newborns (both boys and girls) are passed through a coiled vine and given a name. Some also pierce the infant's ear lobe.

Levirate Marriage

Like the Pathans, Chiang and Karen, the Shinlung practiced levirate marriage. If there is no heir, a widow must marry her dead husband's unmarried brother, and the firstborn son is named after the deceased. There is no ceremony to release the widow (as in the Jewish custom of

Halitza). If the brother refuses to marry her, she may marry anyone. (It is unclear whether this is still practiced.)

Divorce

Marriages are arranged through a matchmaker. In case of a crisis in a marriage, the matchmaker intervenes to clarify the problems. If the wife committed adultery and there are two witnesses to her offense, she is sent away in great shame. According to their tradition, she will be eaten by a tiger from the forest. If the husband committed adultery, he will be eaten by a bear. If there is a disagreement between them on the facts, the matter will be brought before the judges, where the chief sits, and another 12 judges at least (up to 24 judges). In the case of corroboration, the sentence is shunning or banishment. There are eight types of divorces according to different situations and for different reasons. Generally, divorce is avoided.

Menstruation

During menstruation, the woman is forbidden to lie with her husband. If it is discovered that this offense has been committed, the husband is fined an amount equal to the dowry that he received at the time of the marriage.

During menstruation a woman is allowed to wash only her face. She must examine herself throughout her menstruation and must announce that she is menstruating. She is permitted to prepare food during menstruation. On conclusion of menstruation (without any days of purification, as is the Jewish custom) she immerses herself and washes her clothes.

Modesty

Women are not involved in men's affairs. They cover their heads. They are forbidden to wear men's clothing. They sit separately from the men also during worship and they must honor their husbands.

Clothing – Tallit

The Sons of Ephraim are a group within the Shinlung tribe. Like the Pathans, who have a holy garment (Joy-Namaz) that resembles a *tallit*, the Sons of Ephraim have a garment similar to the *tallit* which they consider holy and capable of vanquishing enemies. This garment, called "Ponapam," has blue threads. A man wearing this garment does not retreat in a war.

Unintentional killer (and intentional?)

There is a special pole in the chief's yard. When someone accidentally kills another person and has not reconciled with the victim's parents, he flees to this pole, and cannot be harmed there. This is also announced by the chief. The killer then becomes the chief's slave for seven years. Some say this is also the case for someone who has killed another person intentionally.

The Thief

The thief must return the stolen object. If he cannot do so, the thief becomes the victim's slave for payment of the amount of the theft. The thief receives a humiliating name, which is a badge of shame for him and his family.

Trespassing

The trespasser deserves death at G-d's hand. (It is unclear how this was interpreted in the past and whether there is any related practice today.)

Death and Burial

When someone dies, family members take care of the body. They are therefore impure and must immerse themselves after the seven-day mourning period. (Some say that they immerse themselves twice daily during the mourning period, in the morning and evening). Food, ashes in the oven and even water in the house of the deceased, are considered unclean and are cast out. (It is possible that cooked food may be eaten outside the home.)

Mourners traditionally flagellate themselves with a branch. People who have heard of the death of a relative purify themselves by washing, and anyone who participated in the burial must be purified. Burial is in the ground; there are family burial pits. Burials are usually performed after sunset. On the anniversary of the death, they visit the grave.

Mourning and Purification of the Home

The mourning period lasts seven days (as is the Jewish custom). Mourners recount praises of the deceased and do not go out to work. Some fast during the seven days. A widow may fast an even longer period for her deceased husband. At the first meal (meal of recovery), the parents of the husband or wife bring the mourners a red cockerel to eat. These relatives prepare also food for the mourners during the seven days. During the seven days, it is customary to visit and comfort the mourners (as is the Jewish custom).

After seven days, the priest comes to the home to expel the spirit of impurity by sprinkling water with a branch on the four corners of the house, or on its four walls, and declaring that the home has been purified.

Tithes

The priest receives a tenth of the fruit of the earth, and this is called tithe in their language.

Some ancient songs related to their past

As noted, songs are their main source of tradition and information about Shinlung history. They have not always understood the songs' meanings. Some meanings of their songs became clear to them after reading the

Bible. There are some, such as Mr. Yossi Chachuak, who know ancient songs without understanding their meaning.

Only during sacrifice, prayer and making an oath may they pronounce the name of G-d, as he was instructed by his father:

"My son do not take G-d's name [in vain],
I am a true priest of Manasseh
But I pronounce G-d's name only at the right time
G-d's name is Y-H (or Za) but do not take it in vain"

They used appellations:

Father in heaven ("Holango")
Eternal Father ("Patian")
Guardian of All ("Huano")
Lord of the Souls ("Talaropa")
Dweller on High ("Hong Havanulung")

During prayer, the priests sang:

"Answer me, answer me, Y'wa
Answer me, answer me, He who dwells on Mount Moriah
Answer me, Answer me, He who dwells in the known Red Sea
Answer me, Answer me, He who dwells on Mount Zion.
I, the priest, the Levite, answer me, Ya, answer me.

The most well-known song is a Passover song:

We must keep the Passover festival
Because we crossed the Red Sea on dry land
At night we crossed with a fire and by day with a cloud
Enemies pursued us with chariots
And the sea swallowed them up
And used them as food for the fish
And when we were thirsty
We received water from the rock.

Other short songs:

1) *Tera[?] our enemies were swallowed in the Red Sea*
2) *In olden days we had a scroll*
   A scroll that was eaten by the wicked "Tuluk" [Chinese] dogs.
3) *We yearn, we yearn for G-d's land*
   We yearn for Zion, Y'wa's city
4) *To enter to enter (**"Lutiltil, lutiltil"**)*
   *To enter Zion (**"Chayona lutiltil"**).*

In an important song there are historic names and places:

"Tera led us,
Efram, Yassak
Moriah [?]
Gakob
Sandtolpoi [Red Sea], Sinai, Shilo
From Chayon we went to Afnistan [Afghanistan?]
And from there to Himalawi [Himalayas?]
From Himalawi to Mongolia
From there to Longadim
And from there to Konamin and Manipur

There are other songs that also clearly show a relation to the Jewish people and the Land of Israel.

The Shinlung today

In 1854, the Baptist Church was established in Kan-Fung-Pi in Manipur by the first American Baptist Mission missionary, W. Pettigrew. In 1910, more missionaries arrived and established churches in Churachandpur. As a result of their pressures, the tribal priest lost his status and the community was subject to Christian influences. The new generation lost the spiritual heritage of their fathers and, to the present day, a certain belief in the Christian Jesus still exists.

As noted, a return to the Torah is occurring as a result of contact with Jews and the freedom of worship. Today there are some 6,000 Shinlung in the two states of India and in Tidim (Myanmar) who observe the commandments as written in the Torah, to the best of their knowledge and under the guidance of Gideon Rey, Shimon Jin and others. These Shinlung, who call themselves "Bnei Menashe", are circumcised, observe the Sabbath and Jewish holidays, pray with *tallit* and use Jewish prayer books. They have built their own synagogues, printed prayer books, and obtained Torah scrolls (not all of which are considered *kosher* by Jewish authorities). A few have phylacteries. On the eve of Passover they gather in families and read the *Haggadah* or from the Bible.

In 1988, the Amishav organization sent a rabbinical court to India and 24 young people and young families formally converted to Judaism and immigrated to Israel. By 1991, some 60 Shinlung had immigrated to and converted in Israel. Another 140 were brought to Israel at the recommendation of the late Rabbi Menahem Mendel Schneerson, and all have integrated well. Many of the young people have married with native Israelis or immigrants. Several families acquired greenhouses in Gush Katif and are making good progress in all fields of life.

To date, some 800 "Bnei Menashe" Shinlung have been absorbed in Israel. It is important to emphasize that in India, most of the Shinlung enjoy a middle class standard of living, many working in agriculture. Among those who have immigrated to Israel are college graduates, professionals, and a former minister of tourism. In Israel, the new immigrants face a lengthy absorption process, the challenge of a new language and financial obstacles.

The goal of the Amishav organization is to bring the remaining members of the Bnei Menashe community to Israel as soon as possible, working in full coordination with the Chief Rabbinate of Israel, the Interior Ministry and other relevant authorities.

In November 2002, Amishav opened the Amishav Hebrew Center in Aizawl, Mizoram. The Center's objective is to increase knowledge and understanding of Jewish tradition and history and to help the Bnei Menashe prepare for a complete return to the Jewish people and the Land of Israel. The Center is staffed by a young Bnei Menashe couple who were educated in Israel as well as by rabbis and teachers sent as official Amishav emissaries. Some 350 Bnei Menashe men, women and children study Hebrew and Judaism at the Center each year. Amishav plans to open additional centers in Mizoram and Manipur.

Some of the above information on the Shinlung was taken from a booklet which they themselves published. At the end of this publication, they write:

> *According to the law of the independent State of Israel, which was declared in 1948, every Jew is permitted to return to Israel. Therefore we ask you, good people with good will and deep understanding, to take immediate steps to allow us as Jews to be granted this right and privilege. We, the undersigned, ask to have our rights recognized, and to be allowed to return to our ancestral home according to the law of the State of Israel.*

THE CHIANG-MIN TRIBE IN CHINA

History and Way of Life

The "Chiang" tribe lives in the northwestern Chinese state of Szechwan, near the Tibetan border, in a beautiful mountain area with unique flora and fauna. Since they live above the "Min" Valley they are also called Chiang-Min. They live in fortified villages and were very powerful until they were subjugated by the Chinese.

In the past, this tribe numbered many millions and ruled over a vast area of China, influencing China with its culture and beliefs. Today the tribe numbers a quarter of a million and is a minority in Szechwan. It has its own language but retains little else of its past culture.

According to Chiang tradition, they are children of Abraham. They believe their forefather had 12 sons. They also believe they originated in the Mediterranean and that their journey to China took three years and three months. They have lived in China for about 2,300 years.

At the beginning of the twentieth century, the tribe converted to Christianity under the influence of missionaries, principally the Bishop T. Torrance of Scotland. Much of the information about the Chiang-Min was taken from his book[10] and articles he published in the 1920s.

Torrance considered the Chiang to be Hebrews, from the ancient Hebrews who influenced Chinese culture. He was greatly impressed by their faith, spirituality and moral lifestyle, and wrote about them in a book about the first missionaries in China.[11]

The Shinlung (Manasseh) in India and Myanmar, and the Karen in Myanmar (and perhaps also the "Shan") may originate from the Chiang, since these tribes have a tradition of flight from China and of a lost book apparently taken from them by the Chinese. Likewise, all these people

---

10   Rev. T. Torrance, *China's First Missionaries: Ancient Israelites*, 1937
11   *Ibid.*

have similar rituals. The Chinese subjugated the Chiang after protracted wars, and they fled to the southern regions of China and nearby countries.

Notably, some Chiang have a Semitic appearance. However, following many wars and some victories over the Chinese in the past, they intermarried, and most have a Chinese appearance.

The character traits of this people include integrity, love of their neighbor, mutual aid, loving-kindness, generosity, modesty, gratitude, shyness and stubbornness, like the tribes in Myanmar and India. They live according to high ethical standards, and are also G-d-fearing.

Faith and Religious Practice before Conversion to Christianity

Before the arrival of Christian influence, the Chiang believed in one G-d and considered the Chinese to be idolaters.

They called G-d "Abachi" (The Father of the Spirit), "Mabichu" (The Spirit of Heaven), and "Tian" (Heaven). As a result of Chinese influences, they also called him "G-d of the Mountains," as the mountains were the central place for worship. They saw G-d as omnipotent, watching over all his creatures, judging the entire world fairly, rewarding the righteous and punishing the wicked. This G-d gave man the opportunity to do repentance and gain atonement for his actions. In time of trouble they, like the Karen people (may still) call him "Y'wa".

Like the Karen and Shinlung tribes, the Chiang lived a special way of life centered around the offering of sacrifices. It was forbidden to worship statues or foreign gods, and anyone offering a sacrifice to other gods was subject to death. As a result of Chinese influences, they came to believe in spirits and demons, but did not worship them.

In the past they kept books and parchment scrolls. Today they keep oral traditions. They do not understand many of their own songs and prayers.

Present-day Sacrifices

Offering sacrifices is the focus of religious life for the Chiang-Min. This worship is performed in two ways:

1. **Public sacrifices** – on stone altars built on platforms erected on mountaintops. The altars are constructed of natural stones, without using tools.

2. **Domestic or personal sacrifices** – on domestic altars built on the flat roofs of their houses.

There is an atmosphere of holiness in all these sacrifices, performed by priests whose priesthood is passed from father to son. The priests wear clean white clothes and perform the sacrifices in a state of purity.

Purity is attributed to the Creator, and is required of all men. Sinners and those who are impure may not take part in the worship.

The Chiang-Min do not have statues or images, but they do have two symbols of holiness: a clean white sheet of paper, and a piece of natural white stone. These symbolize absolute purity and, perhaps, the written parchment that they once possessed. Before worshipping G-d, one must become holy and purify oneself. Before offering sacrifices, they bathe, wash their clothing and don clean garments. The sacrificial animal must also be washed and purified.

There is a special place next to the public platforms used for washing and purification by immersion. Anyone who has not purified himself may not approach the place of the sacrifices.

Perhaps as a result of past Assyrian influences, they always try to build their altars next to trees. The altar itself is built of earth and stones laid one on top of the other without being fashioned or cut by any tool. The main part of the service, particularly for a public sacrifice, is performed at night (this, perhaps, to conceal the service from any Chinese onlookers, or just because of the special silence and tranquility of the night).

The elders and the priest place their hands on the head of the sacrifice before it is slaughtered, and then offer prayers.

The purposes of sacrifice are atonement and to bring G-d's blessing on those who offer the sacrifices. The sacrifice itself atones for sin. Blood must be sprinkled on the corners of the altar in order for one to be granted atonement and for one's prayers to be accepted.

In the past there were burnt offerings. Today the sacrifices are generally for payment of vows and for atonement. At the time of the sacrifice, they place 12 flags, to show their origin in the father of 12 sons [of Jacob?]. They believe in a general atonement in the future, after which sacrifices will be annulled.

The Priests

The priests are the religious leaders and conduct the sacrificial worship of G-d. They perform marriages and burials and so forth.

As noted, the priesthood is passed down from father to son. The priest may not perform sacrifices without being ordained in a special ceremony in which sacrifices are also offered.

Unmarried men may not become priests.

The sacrificial ceremonies are performed to the accompaniment of prayers and drums. The priests wear special white garments, a sash and a special head-turban.

By prayer, the priests assert their faithfulness to G-d and observance of G-d's commandments. They try to achieve closeness to G-d by prayer and religious observance.

During prayer the priest includes the following petition:

> *Priests of G-d, you are the priests of the generations who are witnesses to the fact that our sacrifice is pure, and has not been altered by us, but has been performed in the same manner since ancient times. We hereby fulfill our vows. We have not eaten impure food for three days, and we have not been in any impure places. We have gathered in the holy grove, the bundles of grass for the sprinkling of the blood are in their places, we have brought the sacrificial ewe, and we have lowered the rope around the bundles of grass for the sprinkling of the blood. We are about to slaughter the ewe on earth. G-d of the Heavens, at the hour of our sacrifice to You, father of the Spirit, we beg You to descend and come to our grove.*
>
> *If our garments were impure, we would not dare to wear them.*

If our shoes were not pure, we would not dare to wear them. If our hats were impure, we would certainly not wear them. If our backs were not pure, we would not carry the drums on them. If our hearts were not pure, we would not dare to carry out our vows, and to offer up our prayers. The grass has been tied into bundles for the sprinkling of the blood. We offer the bread and the wine before our G-d. We ask You to consider the slaughterer and the priest as sinless! We ask you to absolve the sins of all who are gathered here. We sprinkle the blood in order to atone for our sins. We ask of You, G-d to accept our prayers!

Following this prayer, the head, heart, liver and kidneys are burned with the meat in the fire. The priest receives the shoulders, chest, legs, and skin of the animal.

The meat is divided among the worshippers. A stranger may not partake of it, as the meat is considered holy.

The intestines and entrails are cut up and eaten with unleavened bread. Each worshipper also drinks a small glass of wine.

Other Customs

Funerals and Burials – The deceased is either buried or cremated. A wooden bird is placed on the coffin to symbolize the ascension of the soul to heaven. Two cockerels are brought to the funeral; one is slaughtered and the other left alive. The ceremony is conducted by the priest.

Purification of the soil – In order to request help from G-d for the harvest, a sacrifice is offered at the time of preparation of uncultivated land.

First fruits – The first fruits are brought to the priest.

Safekeeping of the home – To ensure the safety of the house, a ceremony is conducted in which blood is sprinkled on the doorpost and on the mezuzot.

Levirate marriage – When a man dies, his brother marries the widow.

This custom is strictly forbidden by decree of the Chinese authorities, and bears a severe penalty.

Head covering – It is considered shameful for a woman to leave her hair uncovered. The women wear white scarves.

Mixed dancing – Men and women do not dance together.

Closing off forests – They close off forests for 50 years, after which they have a special ceremony to mark their re-opening.

Holidays – On the first day of the tenth month, they celebrate the New Year by offering a sacrifice, which is burnt completely. The Festival of Peace is observed in the middle of the summer. The Festival of Thanksgiving is observed in the fall.

Naming the child – Before the fortieth day of the child's life, a white fowl is slaughtered in the child's honor, and the child is named.[12]

Amishav contact with Chiang

In 1998, the author, Micha Gross and Hillel Halkin traveled to Szechuan Province, China to investigate the connection between the Chiang-Min, Karen, and Shinlung peoples.

At a Chiang-Min teachers' conference, the author and Micha Gross met teachers and a college president who told about the continued practice in villages of animal sacrifice with Israelite elements, as described by Torrance in his articles and books. After the conference, one teacher told the Amishav delegation that he had heard that, of the tribes taken from Jerusalem to exile, one tribe was lost – and that tribe is the Chiang-Min. Furthermore, when asked to explain the discrepancy between the author's calculation that the Chiang should number today about 8 million, when in fact they number only about 1/4 million, the teacher explained that in the past many Chiang migrated south to Thailand, Burma, Bangladesh and India and are now known by other names. Curiously, both the Keren and the Shinlung have a tradition of Chinese ancestry.

12   *Ibid.*

THE TRIBES OF ISRAEL – IN JAPAN [13]

Direction of the wandering Ten Tribes

As noted, the Ten Tribes were exiled to northeast of the Land of Israel, and the texts indicate that they went eastwards, as for instance in Isaiah (43): "I will bring your seed from the east"; or in Jeremiah (3): "In those days the house of Judah shall walk with the house of Israel, and they shall come together out of the land of the north..." Namely, some were exiled to the cities of the Medes (which is rather north than east), and most were exiled to the East, to areas now known as Afghanistan, Pakistan, and Kashmir; after which, they migrated to China, Myanmar and northeast India.

Thus, the Chiang-Min, Karen (the Shan), and Shinlung are peoples connected to China, and together they number over 7 million. The prophecy of Isaiah foretells the return of exiles from all corners of the globe, and especially the Ten Tribes: "Behold, these shall come from afar...these from the north and from the west and these from the land of Sinim".[14]

The 'far isles' in Biblical prophecy

The Japanese islands had no contact with Judaism, Christianity and Islam, but continued to practice idolatry until the modern age. According to Biblical prophecy, especially after the war of Gog and Magog when the

---

13 Most of the information in this chapter is based on Rabbi E. Avichail's visit to Japan and talks with the scholar Mr. Morauka, and also on the following books: The Otzar Israel Encyclopedia; Zonenshein: New Light From Zion; J. Eidelberg: The Japanese and the Ten Lost Tribes of Israel, and others.

14 Isaiah 49.

hand of G-d will be revealed in miracles, faith will spread even to idol-worshippers in distant Asia and the islands of Japan, and the lost and scattered will return.

The following verse in Isaiah 66 may refer to these peoples:

> "...The isles far off, that have not heard My fame, neither have seen My glory; and they shall declare My glory among the nations; And they shall bring [back] all your brethren ... out of all nations...to my holy mountain Jerusalem"[15]

One interpretation of the verse is that there are many descendants of the Ten Tribes in Japan and the men of the "far isles" will bring them back to Israel. Another interpretation is that the men of the 'far isles' (under the great influence of G-d's glory) will bring to Israel descendants of the Ten Tribes from *all* the nations.

Given the ambiguity of the verse, we should clarify whether signs of Judaism exist in Japan, as were found in other countries of the East. In other words, is there evidence that the Japanese, or at least some of them, are descendants of the Ten Tribes?

Tradition by Pictures

According to a collection of various books written decades ago on the subject,[16] there is a Japanese tradition, found particularly among the Samurai, that they came to Japan from the Near East. As proof, some Japanese refer to ancient lacquer paintings found in Shinto temples. These pictures, containing objects that exist in the Near East and not in Japan, depict the wanderings of the first Japanese Emperor Jimmu Tenno and his people in the year 660 BCE. In one painting, there are numerous camels and the Emperor rides a mule. In another, Emperor Jimmu Tenno, his ministers and slaves are seated in a barge, gripping oars; their weapons

---

15   Isaiah, 66:19-20.
16   See note 91 above.

are similar to those found in Assyrian paintings: shields, spears, bows and arrows.

The family of the present emperor of Japan own ancient silk paintings, inherited from their forefathers, which depict men of a Semitic appearance and vessels of the Israelite Temple.

The Shinto Temple

One reason that has led Jews to think that the Japanese might be from the Ten Tribes is the Shinto Temple and ceremonies. (Shinto is the prevailing religion today in Japan.) Shinto temples have an interesting and unique structure that does not exist elsewhere in the world except for the Jewish Temple. The structure of Shinto temples is based on three degrees of holiness: an area accessible to all, an area accessible to the priests alone, and an area accessible only to the high priest.

At the entrance to a Shinto temple is a basin and utensil for washing hands. The basin looks like a trough filled with water. Inside the temple is a Holy Ark, also called "shrine of the book" (although it is not known whether there is today any book there). The (Shinto) holy ark has carrying handles, indicating that it was once carried into battles, as was the Ark in the Jewish tabernacle.

On the temple altar they make only rice offerings and wine libations. Each day they change the offerings and what remains is thrown away. People also bring first fruits and priestly gifts, and hang written petitions inside the temple.

The priests wear short linen pants and long tunics with belts, or a shirt and skirt. They go bareheaded.

The high priest has a special garment that distinguishes him from the other priests. Every day he enters the temple to pour out wine. When he enters he rings a special bell, claps his hands, prays and gives alms.

Antiquities

In addition to the paintings mentioned above, some testimonies indicate that there is a special holy room in the Mikado Palace containing Jewish symbols: broken tablets, a jar (the manna) and a rod (Aaron). There is also a holy mirror on which is written in Hebrew "I Am that I Am", and a sword on which is written "The Lord's is the Salvation". An ordinary person is not allowed to enter this room.

One of the three holy books that the Japanese have is a book that no one has yet been able to decipher. The Japanese say the script is the writing of G-d.

There are ancient monuments in Japan with statues that resemble a Jew wearing a *tallit*.

On the small island Oagi, in a hotel garden (about 1 hour's drive from Kyoto), there is a stone ark inscribed in Hebrew.

In Kyoto, in the old area in which the members of the Hada tribe live, there is a well inscribed with the Japanese word: "Israel".

The Japanese professor Ahiah offers ancient songs as proof of the Hebrew origin of the Japanese. The songs are written in Hebrew and therefore not even understood by the Japanese. There are approximately 50 such songs. They are mentioned also by Mr. Eidelberg in his book "The Japanese and the Ten lost Tribes of Israel."[17] Mr. Eidelberg writes that there are 3,000 Hebrew words in the Japanese language and that some Japanese letters resemble letters in the ancient Hebrew script.

The admiration of the Japanese for the six-pointed star of David is also considered a sign of their Jewish origin.

Jewish customs

Circumcision – Jewish refugees from Vilna during the Holocaust saw in a public bath that most Japanese were circumcised. Mr. Morauka Da Soka, a personal friend of Mr. Mikasonomia, brother of the Emperor of Japan, related that the royal family circumcised their sons on the eighth day, although today only the Emperor's sons are circumcised.

---

17   Joseph Eidelberg, *The Japanese and the Ten Lost Tribes of Israel*, 1980, Sycamore Press, Israel

Menstrual impurity – A menstruating woman is impure. During menstruation, a woman will eat alone and will not prepare food for others. Following menstruation, she is purified with natural water, such as from a spring or the sea. Today women usually bathe in a bathtub following menstruation.

Purity and impurity – An impure man may not enter a holy place. Anyone entering a room where a dead person is laid must purify himself by sprinkling salt on his head (this is not a Jewish custom). Food and clothes in the house of the dead become impure and are discarded.

Purification of the dead – The dead are washed, their hair and nails are cut, and they are wrapped in burial cloth. A candle and a glass of water are placed next to the deceased, and someone sits by the deceased 24 hours.

Funeral and burial – In the past, the deceased was placed in a wooden coffin and buried in the ground. (Today, in order to conserve space, the government requires cremation.) After the burial, mourners traditionally return by a different path from that taken into the cemetery (similar to the Jewish custom). After returning from the cemetery, mourners remove their shoes and sit on the ground (this custom is practiced even today in the village of Shiga) – like the Jewish custom.

Mourning – For two days, mourners eat only food brought to them by relatives (they do not prepare food for themselves). Mourners are not spoken to. For seven days they do not work, and for 49 days they do not eat meat, drink wine or listen to music.

Japanese calendar – In the past, the lunar calendar was used. Today they use the Gregorian calendar.

Tabernacles holiday – On the fifteenth of the first month (the month "Mutzaki"), members of the Hada tribe go into the street carrying various plants. They also sit in huts. On this holiday, they use ancient drawings depicting an altar with Jewish-looking priests offering incense and other ancient drawings.

Phylacteries – Some claim to have seen phylacteries on the heads of Japanese at prayer. Among the Yamabushi tribe, they place a small silver, gold or black hat on their forehead, held by a strap. The Yamabushi tribe belongs to the "Shingon-Shu" sect.

Fringes – Some claim that the priests' clothes have fringes, called "Choya" in Japanese. The author witnessed priests wearing a wide-sleeved shirt with long strings used for tightening the sleeves.

Redemption of the firstborn – According to a certain source, the Japanese have a custom of redemption of the firstborn.

Blood revenge – Is practiced, as was once the Jewish custom.

Honoring one's parents – Parents must be honored and obeyed, on threat of expulsion from the family. However, obedience is required only if the parents' demands do not conflict with G-d's commandments.

Conclusion

The proofs are impressive and also generally well-founded. From all the proofs it is difficult *not* to conclude that there may be a connection between the Japanese, or at least some of them, and the lost Ten Tribes. The love for the Jewish people expressed by over one hundred thousand Japanese also must be taken into account.

In 1985, as part of other activities of the Amishav organization, the author visited Japan to investigate the possible connection of the Japanese to the Jewish people. The research was undertaken by the writer with the assistance of Mr. Sadao Ohara of Okinawa, who had lived in Israel for some eight years with his family and believed in this connection. Mr. Ohara was present at all the visits and meetings with people and exhibits, in temples and museums, including the important conversation with Mr. Mikasonomia, brother of the Emperor of Japan.

In 1991, relations were established with Amishav by a group from Japan that later established the Association of the Ten Tribes. Some meetings were held in Israel between the author and this group, during which for many hours they discussed traditions, history and the many Jewish signs among the Japanese. The group funded the translation into Japanese of the author's book "Judaism".

Since 1991, the Association of the Ten Tribes has partially abandoned Christianity, and now identify with the Christian group "Jews for Jesus" (to the strong condemnation of the author). Apparently they have also begun to observe Jewish commandments and Jewish worship.

THE TEN TRIBES IN KURDISTAN AND THE CAUCASUS (CITIES OF THE MEDES)

According to the books of Kings and Chronicles, the Ten Tribes were exiled by the Kings of Assyria to the cities of Medes and other places.

As explained previously, most descendants of the Ten Tribes live as Gentiles, with signs of Jewishness, to the east of the Land of Israel (or in the northeast): "I will bring your seed from the east".[18] Many will return from China (the land of Sinim).[19] There are some 35 million descendants of the Ten Tribes living in Afghanistan, Pakistan, Kashmir (India), China, Myanmar and India. It is written that these will reunite with Israel at the end of days: "And David my servant shall be their prince".[20]

That they live as Gentiles can be learned from Hosea:[21] "Ephraim has mixed himself among the peoples;" from the Babylonian Talmud, where the Amora Shmuel says: "who made them as complete gentiles;"[22] and in particular, from the Jerusalem Talmud: "they are righteous converts in the future".[23] These sources refer to those who were exiled to "Habor, Hara and the Gozan River".[24] (The Talmud implies that all these localities are in the same region).

A small part of the Ten Tribes, namely part of the tribe Dan (whose portion was in the coastal region), lives in exile and partially observes

18   Isaiah 43:5.
19   Isaiah 49:12.
20   Ezekiel 37: 25.
21   7:8.
22   Yevamoth 160.
23   Sanhedrin 10, 6.
24   Chronicles I, 5.

Judaism from the written law only. Eldad Hadani[25] recounts that when the kingdom was divided, and the Kingdoms of Ephraim and of Judah were preparing for civil war, members of the Dan tribe (those who lived on the coastal plain) decided not to go to war. In order to avoid being attacked by the tribes of the newly-created kingdom of Israel, the Danites moved to Egypt. From there they continued along the Nile to present-day Ethiopia. They are called "Beta Israel" and number today approximately 100,000.

In the opinion of the Gaon of Vilna, the expression "I will assemble her that is lame"[26] refers to these exiles, since they have only the written law (one unstable foot). According to his commentary, the first part of the "Sound a great horn" blessing also refers to them.[27]

Today, most of the Dan tribe has returned to Israel. Because they had a history of continuous practice of Judaism, the Jews of Ethiopia were generally accepted as Jews. However, because of specific problems related to marriage laws, the Chief Rabbinate requires that they undergo a symbolic conversion, or "return to Judaism," by ritual immersion and formal acceptance of Jewish law. (They are already circumcised.)

The third group, discussed in this chapter, are descendants of the Ten Tribes who were exiled to "the cities of Medes" (and perhaps to "Lahlah" – "which is Halazon" – Halwan?) and who continued to live (completely) as Torah-observant Jews.

Where are the Cities of Medes?

The Bible and the Talmudic Sages indicate that Media extended northwest of Persia in an area that included the Kurdistan Mountains, south and west of the Caspian Sea and the Caucasus Mountains between the Black Sea and the Caspian Sea. The capital of Media was Achmetha (present-day Hamadan).

---

25   Version 2.
26   Micah 4:6.
27   Avnei Shlomo, Sound a Great Horn, and see Eldad Hadani, Version 2.

In addition to areas west of the Land of Israel, the Assyrian Empire conquered distant provinces in the lands of Medes and even east of Persia (present-day Afghanistan). Those banished from Israel were exiled to these places in three different stages.

At the time of King Ahasuerus, Jews and Israelites lived in Persia and Media, under a covenant and with the agreement of the authorities.

As noted, this area was included in Greater Media, to which the Kings of Assyria exiled some of the Ten Tribes: "And the King of Assyria carried Israel away unto Assyria and put them in Halah, and in Habor, on the river of Gozan, and in the cities of the Medes".[28]

Part of this area close to the Caspian Sea might already have been called "Casiphia" in Biblical times. Ezra the Scribe sent emissaries to this region to find Levites for the Temple worship: "And I sent them with commandment unto Iddo the chief at **the place Casiphia**; and I told them what they should say unto Iddo [and] his brother, who were set over **the place Casiphia**, that they should bring unto us ministers for the house of our G-d."[29] The Greek scholar Eratosthenes wrote: "The Caucasus mountains were called Casipheos by the natives".[30]

Relations with the Israelites in Media continued for generations. During the Temple period, Rabbi Gamliel sent a letter to Media in connection with the leap year: "And take this letter and write to those in exiled in Babylon and our brethren in Media, and the other exiles of Israel".[31]

There are Talmudic references to Sages who came from Media. The most famous of these, "Nahum the Mede" is mentioned in the Mishna, Tractate Shabbat, Chapter 2. The relationship with the Sages of Israel is particularly important to the process. Sages traveled between the Land of Israel and Media. *Inter alia*, mention is made of Rabbi Akiva's journey to Ginzak in Media: "Rabbi Akiva gave a sermon on the Flood Generation at Ginzak in Media".[32] Other sources refer to Sages such as Rabbi Zadok,

28   Kings II 18:11.
29   Ezra 8: 17.
30   Strabo XI, 2, Book 15.
31   Sanhedrin 11.
32   Bereshit Rabba 33, Avoda Zara 34, 39.

whose father died in "Ginzak of Media,"[33] Rabbi Isaac[34] and Mar Ukva.[35] (The existence of the qualifying detail "of Media" implies that there was another Ginzak, not 'of Media'. Indeed, another Ginzak is mentioned in relation to the Gozan River in Yevamoth 17 and Kiddushin 92 and is, according to the Saadia Gaon, located in northern Afghanistan. The Gozan River, also called the Amu-Daryah, flows today along the northern border of Afghanistan.)

Thanks to contact with the Talmudic and Mishnaic sages, Jewish observance was maintained by the exiles throughout Media – from Kurdistan, Armenia, Georgia, Azerbaijan and Dagestan up to Central Asia (Uzbekistan and Bukhara).

The Maharal of Prague interprets the Midrash in the following way:

> *The Ten Tribes were scattered in three exiles: one was exiled to the Sambatyon, and one past the Sambatyon .... and one to the border of Rivlata*[36] *– there were three kinds of exiles: one by distance – they are exiled afar; ... and the second not only by distance, there are also obstacles between them and from the place from which they were exiled.*[37]

Hence, one exile of the Ten Tribes is distant from Jewish population centers, but nothing prevents access to them; namely, relations are maintained between the main Jewish population centers and these exiles. The contact is not easy to maintain and sometimes certain information, such as the death of Rabbi Zadok's father, arrived only after 3 years. However, because of the continuing relationship with the Jewish leadership during the codification of the Oral Law, this part of the Ten Tribes was saved from assimilation.

---

33 Semakhot 12, Moed Katan 20.
34 Nazir 34.
35 Taanit 11.
36 Yalkut Shimoni II 469, according to Pesikta Rabbati, and in a slightly different version in the Jerusalem Talmud, Sanhedrin, 10: 5-6.
37 Netzah Israel 34.

On the other hand, this is not true for most of the Ten Tribes whose members eventually converted to Islam or Christianity, usually voluntarily, because of their scant knowledge of the Torah, and were therefore cut off from the Jewish people. These are the "obstacles" likened to the "Sambatyon", which will be difficult to cross until the End of Days.

It seems that the part of the Ten Tribes banished to the distant cities of the Medes also suffered assimilation, generally by forced conversions, as will be shown below. In this, its fate is similar to that of the exiled Jews who were forcibly converted in Spain, Mashad and elsewhere. It is our duty to save these brethren, just as it is our duty to save every Jew. Therefore, it is important to investigate and identify the forced converts of the cities of the Medes.

In order to identify the Ten Tribes in this exile, and their brethren who were forcibly converted, we should identify: the countries presently located in the area of the cities of the Medes, the traditions of the Ten Tribes in these places, and the peoples in these countries that have an Israelite past.

Kurdistan

Most of present-day Kurdistan is located within the boundaries of ancient Media: the northern border, the Murat River and Mount Ararat. The southern border of Kurdistan crosses the Mesopotamian Plain and the Khabur Valley to the Euphrates River. Also located in Kurdistan are the areas north of the river plain and the mountains north of the Tigris River. The political borders of Kurdistan are Armenia to the north and Syria to the northwest. The region of Kurdistan includes lands claimed by Iraq, Turkey and Iran.

The Jews of Kurdistan have no documents linking them to the area. However, they do have a widespread oral tradition that they are descendants of the Ten Tribes exiled from the Land of Israel by the Kings of Assyria. There is also a tradition that they have been in Kurdistan since the time of Ezra the Scribe. A few associate themselves with the tribe of Benjamin.[38]

Emissaries from the Land of Israel in Kurdistan were afraid to visit Jews in remote and dangerous regions, staying only in the large Jewish communities. They did send local Jews to collect charitable contributions,[39] and managed to maintain relations with these small communities.

Some of the non-Jewish Kurds in Kurdistan may also be descendants of the Ten Tribes. This is implied by the Talmudic Sages when they say that they "accept converts from the Kurds".[40] In order to avoid problems arising from forbidden marriages, even though they are of the seed of Israel, "they were made as Gentiles" (they had become as Gentiles so they must convert).

The neighbors of the Jewish Kurds are Assyrians, also called Nestorians, many of whom were Jews converted to Christianity during the first and second centuries. Their origin is in the early Eastern Syrian church whose seat was in Edessa in Syria. They use Syrian Aramaic like the Knanites, but have preserved many Jewish precepts.[41]

Armenia

Armenia (its ancient name in Babylonian and Aramaic was Ararat) was once part of Greater Media. Today, the land is divided between Turkey and Iran. It was once divided in two: Armenia Major, bordering the Taurus Mountains in the south, the Caspian Sea in the north and Persia (Iran) in the east; and to the west, Armenia Minor (Cilicia) – today's Harput district.

Biblical and Talmudic sources indicate that the Ten Tribes were exiled to Armenia and from there wandered north to the Caucasus:

---

38   See Otzar Israel Encyclopedia and the Hebrew Encyclopedia.
39   Ohalei Yaakov, p. 140.
40   Yevamoth 16.
41   See Kasdai, pp. 4-13.

Of the Ten Tribes it is said: "And you shall be cast into Harmon",[42] *and in Targum Yonatan it is written "Harmeni" corresponding to Armenia. The story, concerning redemption of captives, of Rabbi Tanhum son of Rabbi Hiya, may well refer to this: "They redeemed captives **from Armon".***[43]

The conquerors of Babylon are also "from the Kingdoms of Ararat, Minni and Ashkenaz",[44] and, according to Targum Yonatan, they are "Ara Kardo [Kurdistan], Hormani [Armenia?] and Hadayev [former Assyria]". In Midrash Eikha Rabbati, the name Armenia is explicit:

*'The burden of my sins was placed in His hand' – he persevered how to bring the evil upon me. He said: If I banish them to the desert they will die of hunger, but if I banish them to **Armenia**, there are cities and districts and food and drink.*[45]

In the Jerusalem Talmud, Rabbi Nahman quotes Rabbi Yaakov **"Armenaya".**[46]

It is interesting to note that, in Armenia, and particularly among the nobility of Armenia Minor, there is a widespread belief among the Christians that they are of Jewish origin. They also have Jewish customs, such as slaughtering animals by the neck, differentiation between pure and impure cattle, fasts similar to Jewish fasts, and laws of menstrual impurity. Unlike other Christians, they do not celebrate Christmas.

In the "History of Armenia" it is said: "all the cities of Armenia and the Caucasus were full of Jews who were exiled there by the Kings of Assyria together with Aram, Damascus to Ashdot, Kavar River."[47]

---

42   Amos 4.
43   Yevamoth 45.
44   Jeremiah 51.
45   Eikha Rabbati I: 44.
46   Gittin 86, 5-7.
47   Algoli and Eliezer Haparpi, Shivtei Yaakov veNetzurei Israel, Z. Kasdai, p. 6.

The Caucasus: Georgia, Azerbaijan and Dagestan

The Caucasus is a mountainous land region between the Black Sea and the Caspian Sea, with Iran and Armenia to the south.

The area is inhabited by a diverse population of some 50 ethnic groups. The major countries of the Caucasus, apart from Armenia, are Georgia, Azerbaijan and Dagestan.

There is a tradition among the Jews of the Caucasus of descent from the Ten Tribes. In 1250 CE, the Dutch priest Rubericos visited a settlement of Jews in Derbent (Dagestan) who told him that they were descendants of the Ten Tribes.[48]

A Christian missionary who visited the Caucasus in 1837-8 also related that the Jews of the Caucasus, as well as some of the non-Jewish peoples of the eastern Caucasus, claim to be descendants of the Ten Tribes.[49] This is reinforced by the resemblance of Jews of Kurdistan to the inhabitants of the Caucasus, and the results of DNA tests.

Peoples in the Caucasus of Israelite origin

Throughout the Caucasus and Georgia, there have been forced conversions of Jews by Moslems and Christians.

In 737 CE, the Jews of the Caucasus were forcibly converted to Islam: "The Arab hero Abu Salim (in 737) brought Islam, and spread it among the Jews of Caucasus and Iberia (Georgia) by his harsh sword, after he forcibly converted them."[50]

Some 200 years later, Musa al Zafrani, know as Abu Amran Al Taflisi (Tibilis) continued the campaign, converting the remnants of the ancient Jews to the Islamic religion.[51]

---

48   Kasdai, p. 79.
49   M. Altschuler, Jews of Eastern Caucasus, p. 344, and also many others. This is also the opinion of scholars Charani, Kasdai and Zuratakov, p. 32. In Altschuler's opinion this is only a conjecture.
50   Kasdai, ibid., p. 17.
51   *Ibid.*

Peoples such as the Ossetes, Chechens, Mingrelians and Lezgians, etc., "and almost all the nations of the Caucasus, are descended from the Israelites, from the exile of the Ten Tribes".[52] Today some of these peoples retain no tradition of their Israelite origin, as the author discovered during a visit to the Caucasus in the summer of 1992.

The ancient name of Georgia is Iberia; in Latin, Iberica. It may be the place to which Mar Zutra refers when, in response to the question as to where the Ten Tribes were exiled, he answers – "Afriki".[53] Interpreters insist that this "Afriki" is not in Africa, but in the direction of the empire of the Kings of Assyria – the area of Greater Media. In the time of Alexander the Great, there were Jews or Israelites in Iberia: "Alexander found in the country of Iberia greatly fortified cities ... Zenob is a place settled by Israelites"[54]

A book of the history of Derbent (Dagestan)[55] is even more far-reaching: "Until the arrival of the Arabs in Iberia and then to the country of Tabaristan and Dagestan, all its inhabitants observed Jewish law and were related to the Israelites".

The writer Kirasinkani, who lived in Tibilis in the mid-fourteenth century, noted: "He found there also eastern Jews, descended from the Assyrian exiles, who believed in the law of Moses and the Prophets etc., and were called among themselves Israelite 'Taplisites'".[56]

It should be noted that there is no *halakhic* significance for "Jews" (the Israelites) living in the areas of Greater Media and that by Jewish law they are considered as any other ordinary Jews. However, in the case of those forcibly converted to Islam, it is a positive commandment and a true need to bring them back to the Jewish people and Jewish law (as for all the forced converts in the world, if possible).

---

52   Kasdai, ibid., Chapter 6, and M. Altschuler, pp. 34-5, 40, 42, 46, 47, 52, 53, 54 and 55.
53   Sanhedrin 94.
54   The Jews and the Slav Language, Vilna, 1867, p. 17.
55   1868, pp. 91-102.
56   Kibret al Anakmar, cited by Kasdai, ibid.

BETA ISRAEL IN ETHIOPIA

As noted, there are three different situations as regards the Ten Tribes. Most live as Gentiles in the East, with signs of Jewishness. A relatively small number, about half a million, live completely Jewish lives in the area of ancient Media (Kurdistan and the Caucasus) and throughout Central Asia.

The third and smallest group, connected to the tribe of Dan, lives in accordance with the written Torah only. In a commentary (attributed to the Gaon of Vilna) to the "Sound a great horn for our freedom" blessing[57] reference is made to those who were exiled to the "mountains of darkness" who have no freedom: "they have only one Torah, the written Torah, and they did not receive the oral Torah"...it is to these that the expression in Micah 4 refers, "I will assemble her that is lame". Therefore, the beginning of the blessing "Sound a great horn for our freedom" was instituted for them.

This tradition of the Gaon of Vilna is supported by the Gaon's predecessors, who speak of this matter, and it recalls "Eldad Hadani" and the "Mordechai".

According to the tradition recorded in "Eldad Hadani", the Dan tribe (that lived in the coastal region), was a strong warrior tribe that went into voluntary exile (when the Israelite Kingdom was divided after King Solomon) because they did not wish to participate in the imminent civil war between the kingdoms of Judah and of Israel. (Indeed, a war was waged later and, according to Chronicles 13, half a million were killed.) They migrated from the Land of Israel to Egypt and continued along the Nile to Ethiopia.

This tradition was supported by the great Sages down the ages. One

---

57 Commentary in "Avnei Eliyahu", Siddur of the Gaon of Vilna.

of the most famous, the *Radbaz*,[58] writes "Those who come from the land of Ethiopia are certainly from the tribe of Dan, and because there were no sages and Cabbalists among them they perceived only the written Law".[59] Another great *halakhist* and a disciple of the *Radbaz*, Rabbi Jacob Kastro, (the *Maharikas*), wrote: "We are commanded to redeem and restore the Ethiopian Jews, although they behave like the Karaites, because they are of the Dan tribes and did not learn from Zadok and Boethus.[60] This opinion was upheld by other Jewish sages, such as Rabbi Ovadia of Bartenura and, in our times, the Gaon Rabbi Ovadia Yossef: "and there is no doubt that these *Gaonim* who determined that they are of the Dan tribe, studied and sought and reached this conclusion according to reliable evidence and testimonies."[61]

In light of this *halakhic* tradition, reinforced by the Chief Rabbi of Israel, the Jews of Ethiopia began to immigrate to Israel. Today their numbers are estimated at some 80,000, including converts to Christianity ("Falashmura"). Most have already reached Israel and become Israeli citizens.[62]

The Amishav Organization possesses extensive information on the subject, and the author addressed Israeli rabbis at the beginning of the mass immigration from Ethiopia, at Beit Ariel in Jerusalem. However, because many other organizations are involved in this matter, Amishav has not taken an active role.

---

58   Rabbi David Ben Zimra (Radbaz) (1479-1573).
59   Responsa Divrei David, Ishut, 5.
60   Erekh Lehem, Yoreh Deah, 158.
61   Letter of Adar I 7, 5733-1973
62   For a detailed discussion see: Rabbi Menahem Waldman, *Me-Ever Le-Naharei Kush* (Beyond the Ethiopian Mountains) and "Me-Etiopia L'Yerushalayim" (From Ethiopia to Jerusalem).

THE DISPERSED OF JUDAH

The Marranos *(Anussim)* of Spain and Portugal
The Knanites in Southern India

THE MARRANOS *(ANUSSIM)* OF SPAIN
AND PORTUGAL

On the First of Tammuz 5151 (1391), "G-d aimed his bow like an enemy at the community of Seville... her gates were set on fire and many of her people were killed; but most gave up their religion and some sold their children and wives to the Ishmaelites... some died for the sanctification of G-d's name and many desecrated the holy covenant."[1] Similarly, in the community of Cordoba, "There were no adults and children left in the community who did not give up their written religion."

In this way, religious persecution spread to Toledo and throughout the entire region. Many Jews were forced to embrace Christianity and even to make a proclamation of faith. The Jews converted by force were called "Marranos," perhaps because of the expression in the New Testament which they were forced to declare – "Maranatha" – to acknowledge the arrival of "the lord" (Jesus), or because of the word's similarity to the Spanish word for pork. The converts were also called "conversos" (new converts) and "christianos nuevos" (new Christians). In the Balearic Islands (Majorca and others), they were called "Chuetas" (the pork eaters) because of their eating pork in public.

Religious conversion as a result of persecution spread throughout Spain. After the expulsion from Spain in 1492, many Jews moved to neighboring Portugal, mainly northern Portugal.

Approximately one hundred years after the beginning of religious persecution in Spain, a decree passed by King Manuel of Portugal (5257/1496) ordered the expulsion of all Jews from Portugal within a period of eleven months. This expulsion resulted from pressures from the Spanish monarchy. King Manuel, whose real desire was for the Jews to

[1] From the letter of Rabbi Hasdai Crescas.

remain, ordered all Jewish children under 14 to be seized and forcibly baptized. Adults were also seized. Consequently, many families decided to give up their religion in order to remain with their children. Many others committed suicide together with their children for the sanctification of G-d's name. On the actual day of the expulsion (ships had been especially prepared in advance) the entire crowd of approximately 20,000 Jews was dragged to "churches", forcibly baptized with water and declared to be Christians. Among the forcibly baptized were the father of the *Ralbah*[2] and the father of Rabbi Joseph Caro.

There were many Marranos in Spain and Portugal. Although some fled to places such as Italy, Turkey or North Africa, a very large number remained in Spain and Portugal. In 1505, a member of the Venetian government who was delayed in Spain claimed that one-third of the urban inhabitants of Spain were descendants of Marranos.[3] At the same time, historian D. Azbo claimed "approximately one-fifth of the inhabitants of Portugal, mainly the city-dwellers, are descendants of Jews." On this basis, another writer expresses the opinion that "every Portuguese who was born outside of a village can be presumed to have Jewish blood flowing in his veins."

The Marranos were divided, generally speaking, into three groups:

1) Those who willingly assimilated among the Gentiles in order to attain important positions in government or to become rich. Among this group were some who fought against their brethren, spoke slander against them, and prevented their return to the Jewish religion[4]. These are considered to have converted willingly.

2) Those who secretly felt a deep connection to the faith of their fathers and a love of Jews. They secretly observed a few of the commandments, but made no effort to leave their land in order to return to the complete observance of Judaism.

---

2   Ralbah: Rabbi Levi Ben Habib, 1483-1545.
3   Graetz.
4   See Ribash (Rabbi Isaac Ben Sheshet Perfet) Responsa No. 11.

3) Those who remained true to their origins, secretly observed all of the commandments, and used all kinds of ruses in order to maintain their observance under difficult circumstances. The Marranos were harshly persecuted by priests, the Church, and the government. Gentiles often instigated pogroms against them. For example, on a single day in 1506, more than 500 Marranos were killed in Lisbon.

According to Jewish Law, the first two groups are considered Gentiles. With regard to the third group, their marriages are not considered valid, because they did not have valid witnesses, and there are therefore no problems with regard to the offspring of illicit marriages (*mamzerut*).

The activities of the Inquisition in both Spain and Portugal brought terrible suffering, degradation, and even death (often by burning) to the Jews and forced many of them to seek refuge in other countries. Unfortunately, the Inquisition often reached beyond the borders of Spain and Portugal. The Inquisition persisted in Portugal over a period of 285 years (from 1532 to 1817). Throughout this entire period, the Jewish tradition was observed in secret. Until the end of the 17th century, there were still many who were familiar with Judaism and Jewish law. This was followed by the gradual fading of the practice of Judaism and familiarity with Hebrew until only a few customs remained. As a result, assimilation became widespread. In many places, especially in northern of Portugal, communities of Marranos remained which did not assimilate, even though their knowledge and practice of Judaism were minimal.

Fifty years ago, Dr. N. Slouche wrote, "An accepted lie existed in the world at large, that the Marranos of Spain and Portugal had become completely assimilated, and that they would never return". Today, it may be said that at least five hundred thousand descendants of the Marranos are living in Portugal. Of these, some still identify with their past and observe some customs and traditions, and there is hope for their return to Judaism.

In contrast to the situation in Portugal, it is very difficult to speak today of clear concentrations of Marranos in Spain. The Inquisition in Spain was far crueler than in Portugal and the possibilities for escape were more plentiful. Therefore, when the Inquisition ended in 1780, there remained no large groups in mainland Spain with a clear tradition of being Jewish, and certainly not of observing Jewish customs.

In the Spanish Balearic Islands, however, there remains a large group of approximately thirty thousand Marranos who were prevented from assimilating. Most of these Marranos lived on the large island of Majorca (approximately 400 km off the east coast of Spain). Until 52 years ago, this group had not been allowed to assimilate. Since then, major changes have occurred; resulting mainly from the change of government in Spain, and this community is becoming smaller and weaker, primarily by choice.

The "Chuetas" (descendants of Marranos) in Majorca can be divided into three types:

1) Those who have remained Catholics and try to prove their faithfulness to Christianity, because of their past suffering and their desire to escape from it;

2) Those who have left religion altogether, as a result of a deep aversion caused by pressures of the Church in the not-too-distant past. This group is also not interested in Judaism, and is active in the Socialist party; and

3) Approximately ten percent of the people, who are interested in learning about their Jewish past and Judaism, and even in returning to Judaism. Some wish to be affiliated with a synagogue, and some are interested in coming to live in Israel.

In Portugal, conditions today are very difficult. The entire population is suffering from economic difficulties as a result of the change of government. Approximately 2.5 million people have left Portugal in order to find a means of supporting themselves in wealthier countries (Germany, France, and others, even Spain). The Marranos of Portugal, despite a more practical connection to Judaism, live like gentiles in an atmosphere of materialism and seek a life of comfort. Some, however, are interested in Judaism and in living in Israel.

From the perspective of Jewish law, all descendants of Marranos are required to undergo, at the very least, symbolic conversion to Judaism.

Amishav established ties and activities with the Marrano community in Belmonte, Portugal in 1981, even before the community was officially formed. This relationship developed through visits of various members of Parliament and students until 1991, when a Jewish community began to take form, headed by several youth under the guidance of Elias Nones. At the urging of various agencies and with the agreement of the Chief Sephardi Rabbi of Israel, Rabbi Mordechai Eliyahu, 63 people were converted by a rabbinical court headed by Rabbi Joseph Sebag and members of Amishav.

Approximately two years later, Rabbi Joseph Sebag returned to Israel. His successor Rabbi Shlomo Sebag continued for a few years, during which the community expanded and grew.

Today, Amishav sponsors a number of full-time emissaries in Portugal and Spain. May it be G-d's will that the promises of "He Who gathers the dispersed of Israel" and "The sons shall return to their borders" be fulfilled.

198

THE KNANITES IN SOUTHERN INDIA
An ancient outpost of Judeo-Christianity
(Including excerpts from the writings of the late M.K. Tomas of Trivandrum)

Ancient Tradition

Kerala, the verdant coastal strip of Southwest India, was an immigrant haven in ancient times. Whoever the original inhabitants were, they were either driven into the lush tropical forests and hill ranges or enslaved to field labor.

It is not known when, or in what order, the immigrant races arrived. Perhaps the first were the snake-worshipping Nagars (origin unknown), who evolved into the warlike 'Nayars', becoming the land-owning and military class and spreading throughout the country. The numerous 'Ezhavas', supposedly of Polynesian origin, may have emigrated via Ezham or Ceylon. They brought with them the Kera Palm (Coconut) which gave the land its name. The 'Nambidiris', Aryan Brahmins, established themselves as the intellectual elite by the seventh century of the Common Era. Numerous other racial groups penetrated the hill ranges and remained minorities and members of the lower classes.

Merchants from Greek and Roman ports, Arabia, Egypt and Palestine were engaged here in the spice trade centuries before the Common Era. The Bible suggests such trade contacts by the Hebraic names for ivory, apes, and peacocks (I Kings 10:22), words of South Indian origin. Even the Hebrew word "apirion" (palanquin) in the Song of Songs is derived from its Indian name. As a result of merchant trade, the coast was fully settled by Roman, Greek and Jewish communities by the late Second-Temple period. Buddhism and Jainism were the dominant religions until the 6th century. With the ascendancy of the Nambidiris and Brahmins, Vedic Hinduism came to the foreground.

Into this whirlpool of race and religion plunged Christianity soon after its appearance on the world stage. A persistent tradition, lacking definite historical evidence, ascribes the introduction of Christianity in Kerala to St. Thomas, a disciple of Jesus, who allegedly landed in Muziris (Shinkli of Jewish lore) in 52 CE. In 'History of the Church', Eusebius refers to Pontaenus, a stoic Philosopher of Hebrew origin and the head of the 'Catechetical' School of Alexandria, who visited India around the year 180. Pontaenus found that Matthew's Gospel (in Aramaic) had arrived before him, and was in the hands of some people there who had come to know Christianity. This implies that he met with either a Jewish or Judeo-Christian group.

In 345 CE, the small Christian community was reinforced by a new group of immigrants. According to tradition, it consisted of Bishop Joseph Rabban, several priests and deacons, and laity (men and women) numbering 400 in all, under the leadership of Knayi Thoma from Nazareth. The community's name (Knanaya or Knanite) is derived from his name. Ancient songs refer to his name in different forms – Thomas Kinan, Knaya Thoma, Thoma Cana, etc. Scholars are not sure whether the name refers to a merchant (Cananeo) or a locality (from Cana).

Knaya Thoma and his people found enough favor with the Ruler (Cherakon or Cheraman Perumal) that they received a Copper Plate – a charter of land, high social privileges and lordship over 18 lower classes, such as barbers, carpenters, bow makers, toddy-toppers, tailors and smiths. The original Copper Plate disappeared with the Portuguese in the 15th century, and may be in the Torro de Tombo in Lisbon, or in an old Franciscan convent in Portugal. There are translations of the manuscript in the British Museum.

Ancient songs of the community commemorate its traditions. However, the versions have been altered due to changes in ecclesiastical allegiance over the course of centuries, so as to cater either to Catholic or Jacobite interests. These altered versions present unreliable traditions about the origin of the community. Knanites are represented as Persian Christians fleeing from persecution under Sapor II, or as an admixture of immigrants from Edessa, Jerusalem, and Mesopotamia. Hints about their true origin can be gleaned from some parts of the songs.

All of the following indicate a definite connection with Judeo-Christian communities in Edessa and Jerusalem: the term used about Thoma, viz. Nazrani (a modified form of the Greek word Nazarene applied to Jewish Christians), the number 72 as the number of families involved (an important number in Jewish lore), reference to head covering (women at prayer covering the head is a Jewish custom), reverence for the Ten Commandments, mention of a gold crown and a six-pointed star (in the description of a bridegroom's dress), and bridal songs reminiscent of the Song of Songs. Land's 'Anecdota Syriaca' states that Thomas Cana is of Jerusalem. Mingana's 'Early Spread of Christianity in India' refers to him as Thomas the Cananite, of Cana which is Jerusalem.

The Knanites are also known locally by the term Thokkumbhagar (Southist). One explanation is that in the City of Mahadovarpattanam, the immigrants settled in the southern part, and other Christians in the northern part. Another connects the term with the North and South Kingdoms of Palestine. Both explanations are unsatisfactory.

In the following pages, an attempt is made to trace the origin of this ancient community from the meager information available.

The Nazarenes (Christians) in Kerala

When the Knanites, or Judeo-Christians, or Nazranis, landed in Krangow in 345 CE, according to the ancient songs, they were met by Jews and small groups of Judeo-Christians who had the Hebrew Gospel. Probably they would have also met groups of Pauline Christians who may have by then reached Kerala. After the grant of the Copper Plate Charter of Privileges, the different groups of Nazarenes (Jewish or Petrine and Pauline) segregated themselves and settled in different parts of Mahadevarpattanam, more or less synonymous with Krangow or Muziris (or Shinkli of the Jews). The Knanites may have chosen the Southern portion and got the name of Southists (or, as some say, Sudhists, which means Puritans). However, there may be greater significance in this term.

Certain suggestions contained in the book 'The Scrolls and Christian Origins' by Mathew Black (1961) may be summarized as follows: Essenes represented an ascetic movement in Israel, a movement represented in ancient times by Kenites, Nazirites, Rachabites, etc. The movement flourished in the post-exilic period as a non-conformist tradition with two main groups, Northern and Southern. From the Northern group came the men of the Qumran Community. A century later, against the background of the Southern group, Jesus proclaimed in Galilee the Gospel of the Kingdom of G-d. However, the Fourth Gospel reveals that Jesus had relations with the Southern group at a later stage.

The Kenites seem to be distant relatives of the Knanites, the non-conformist separatist group in Kerala. The name 'Southists' may point to a very ancient division preserved among Essenes, later among Nazarenes in the Middle East, and transmitted through Edessa to Nazranis in Kerala.

The Knanites who arrived in the 4th century were Nazranis. Over the course of time the term (Nazrani, or Nazarene) came to be applied to all ancient Christians in Kerala. The Edessan Knanites were also called Syrians, and they brought the Syriac liturgy. Thus the total Christian population in Old Kerala also came to be known as Syrian Christians. By the time the Portuguese arrived, the tradition of St. Thomas' apostleship had become widespread and the Portuguese called them St. Thomas Christians.

Beginning in the 5th century, Eastern Christendom came under strong Nestorian influences. Nestorian missionary enterprise was far-reaching and widespread up to Cathay and beyond. Gradually, the Kerala Christians, including Knanites, came under the Nestorian hegemony. Priests and prelates came from the Nestorian and Catholic Patriarchates. When Nestorian power declined from the 13th century, clergy were recruited irrespective of whether they were Nestorian or Coptic or Jacobite. Even clergy from the Roman See were recruited. During this period of fluidity and confusion, the original religious faith took on the hues of whatever mother-church in the Middle East or Egypt happened to send clerical help and attain temporary local dominance. However, like the Essenes and the Nazarenes who were their forebears, the Knanites, while bending to the winds of liturgical change, steadfastly maintained their separate social customs and status. They never mixed socially or intermarried with other Christian sects or pagans; they were rigidly endogamous; and they preserved their Jewish heritage in customs and manners, including some wedding customs. Wedding songs and other ancient songs kept them constantly reminded of their rich heritage.

The Portuguese arrived on the scene by the 16th century. By 1590, supported by Roman Catholicism and with the military assistance of ruling chiefs, they forcibly subjected all Syrian Christians to Rome. Syrian books and records were burned. For 54 years the entire Kerala Christian community was subject to Rome. They rose in revolt, led by a Knanite priest. The majority of parishes seceded from the Roman Catholic fold and made attempts to recruit priests and prelates from non-Roman Catholic sources. By chance, they netted Jacobite help; the Syrian Church initiated relations with the Patriarchate of Antioch from 1653.

Ever since, the Syrian Church in Kerala has been split main into two factions, namely Roman Catholic and Jacobite. The Knanites, although they preserve social uniformity among themselves, stand divided in matters of faith. This division has continued for three centuries and tends to keep the two groups estranged even socially. The religious division is so profound that the two groups, although aware of a common origin and common heritage, are unable to unite.

> The 70 families of Jacob who went to Egypt, multiplied into six lakhs of people of a mixed community within a period of 400 years, until Moses redeemed them.[5] However, our (?) community of 70 families, which settled in Kerala in 345 C.E., has not multiplied into more than two lakhs of people (Catholic and Jacobite together), though more than 16 centuries have passed since we settled in Kerala. This is because we have never wavered from our commitment/tradition not to intermingle or intermarry with gentiles. When we settled in Kerala our language was Aramaic. Although as a spoken language it has completely vanished,

5   Lakh = 100,000 – E.A.

Aramaic is until now used for all religious services. We do not intermarry unless one adopts the other's faith. Further, Knanite churches will not solemnize a marriage ceremony between a Knanite and a follower of another faith, or even another sect of Christianity. In other words, in such matters, too, we are strictly endogamous.

My personal view is that salvation for Knanites lies only in one direction. They have to forcibly eschew the religious trappings imposed by the Roman Catholic and Jacobite Churches, go back to their Judeo-Christian faith in one G-d, and to the doctrine and customs espoused by the Jerusalem Church. The crying need of the hour is for all Knanites to join together. They should consider the divine call for unity of Israel found in Ezekiel 37:15-22 as applicable to them, mutatis mutandis. Before this can be achieved, the Knanite youth should undertake a study of their history, of the history of Jews and Judeo-Christians. Much study and research are called for. They should seek the help of historians of whatever faith in India and abroad, including Israel, in order to reconstruct their past. To this end, the writer hopes this article will serve as a humble pointer. (M.K. Tomas of Trivandrum)

Mr. Tomas was the owner of rubber and coconut plantations in Kerala who, through study of the Bible, decided to return to Judaism. He translated the Jewish prayer book, as well as numerous other texts that could be helpful for his community's return to Judaism, into his native language, Malayalam. He gained as many as 300 followers.

The author first learned of Mr. Tomas' group by chance during a visit to New Delhi in 1980. The author visited Kerala and spent many hours with Mr. Tomas. The author visited Mr. Tomas again in 1982.

During a visit to Israel, Mr. Tomas met the Chief Rabbi of Israel, Rabbi Shlomo Goren, who agreed to help him complete conversion in Israel, and obtained mezuzot, tallitot, tefilin and other articles to begin observing the *mitzvot.*

Mr. Tomas' dream was to return completely to Judaism and serve as an example for the rest of his people to follow. To this end, he requested the assistance of the Chief Rabbi of Israel. Unfortunately Mr. Tomas died of a serious illness before he could complete his own conversion. Two of his grandchildren formally converted and now live in Israel.

COMMUNITIES SEEKING TO ADOPT JUDAISM

Converts of San Nicandro, Southern Italy
"Bnei Moshe" of Peru
The "Bayudaya" of Uganda
"Ba'Derej Leyerushalaim" of Mexico

THE CONVERTS OF SAN NICANDRO, SOUTHERN ITALY

Many of the Second Temple Period exiles were absorbed in Southern Italy and Sicily. The majority assimilated, but memories of a Jewish past left numerous signs.

A relationship to Judaism may exist deep in the soul even though it offers no external proofs. It may come to the surface in the form of the serious devotion of righteous converts. Such was the case of the "Derej Leyerushalaim" group in Mexico and the "Bnei Moshe" in Peru. Astonishingly, similar groups appeared simultaneously both in southern Italy and Uganda.

The group in southern Italy was discovered in the town of Sannicandro, close to the city of Foggia, then a small village. Sannicandro is located in a mountain region far from any large urban center. There are absolutely no Jews in the region.

Donato Manduzio

Confined to a wheelchair as a result of a leg wound received in the war against the Austrians in 1919, Sergeant Donato Manduzio of Sannicandro was an avid student of a wide range of subjects.

In 1930, Donato Manduzio dreamt that he had been charged with the mission of "lighting a light". It was clear to him that the Bible contained the great light that he was called to disseminate. Within a short time he had organized a group of Bible students in his home. The group grew gradually until it encompassed half the village.

Jewish Life in Sannicandro

Manduzio and his group not only studied but also began to observe the Old Testament commandments as they understood them, arousing bitter opposition from the Roman Catholic Church.

However, in time Manduzio became a respected personage in town, settling all the local disputes justly and honestly, without personal gain. In this way Manduzio and his group gained the positive esteem of their neighbors, and they came to be known in the village as "Bnei Israel" and "our Jews".

From a visitor from Rome, the group learned that Jews were alive and numerous in the world, and that there was a Jewish community in Rome with a chief rabbi, Rabbi David Prato. Excited letters sent to Rome went unanswered, causing the community great sorrow and suffering, even leading them to fast. A relationship was finally established in 1934 when the Italian Chief Rabbi sent his *shamash* (beadle) with prayer shawls, prayer books and Bibles. The beadle prepared the community for three years towards conversion. In 1937, the community received a letter from the Chief Rabbi recommending that they wait for a more propitious time to convert, because of the Italian government's threatening attitude towards Judaism. This situation lasted until the end of World War II.

At the end of World War II, an officer of the Jewish Brigade, Pinchas Lapid, discovered the remote community by chance. Following a number of very emotional meetings, he took upon himself the mission of assisting them, and they were converted.

With the establishment of the State of Israel, the community immigrated to Alma in the Galilee, and from there dispersed throughout Israel. The author visited Sannicandro in 1991, and saw that a very small group remained, mostly women, who continued to live a Jewish life as best they could.

"BNEI MOSHE" OF PERU

The Bnei Moshe is a group of mixed Spanish and South American ethnicity that came into being in 1948 in the city of Cajamarca in Northern Peru, and slowly developed its present Jewish life-style.

Descendants of Marranos lived in Cajamarca and the vicinity in the past, and even today the people of the village of Salandin have a tradition of having arrived in the area with the Portuguese, so it is possible that some of the group have Jewish roots.

The founder of the group, Mr. Segundo Villanueva, subsequently Zerubavel Zedekiah, was introduced to Judaism at the age of 15, when he received a gift of the Bible from his father, who exhorted him to study it, because it contained the truth. Study of the Bible gradually brought him to reject Catholicism and, together with his brother Alvaro (today Mordechai Meir), he became an Evangelist, observing the Sabbath and *Kashrut*. This became easier when in 1954 they joined a vegetarian community in Cajamarca.

As they studied and increased their knowledge of the Bible, the Villanueva brothers realized that they must leave the Evangelists, and they began independent observance. Their following gradually increased, and in 1961 swore to observe all the precepts of the Torah. In 1967, about twenty years after their first steps, the group numbered over 200. Wishing to be removed both from social pressures and foreign influences, they decided to form a community (a kind of kibbutz) in the Amazon jungle to study Judaism and practice *Torah* observance.

In 1969 first contact was made with Rabbi Abraham Ben Hamu, the Sephardic Rabbi of Lima, who used his limited resources to supply the group with books and other materials on Judaism. Their desire to have themselves ritually circumcised was realized when the Jewish physician Dr. Reuven Kogen agreed to circumcise them in 1971. The decision to undergo circumcision created dissension within the group and led to the departure of many members. In light of the ideological and practical disputes, the group broke up and its members returned to the city. The return to the world from the jungle exacted its price. Members of the group dispersed to various localities throughout Peru. Some returned to Cajamarca under the leadership of Victor Chico. Some moved to Trujillo, and shortly thereafter to the desert region about 8 km from the city Almilagro in order to remove themselves from the Christian environment and to continue living a Jewish life.

Alvaro Villanueva moved to Lima, where he formed a small community with his friend Selirosas. They tried to establish relations with Jews and learn about Judaism. They believed that the practice of Judaism must also lead to immigration to Israel. They received assistance from various Jews, such as the Israeli Ambassador, Mr. Gideon Tadmor (1981). Assistance was also rendered by Jews who passed through the area, and by the engineer, Mr. David Liss of Rishon LeZion, who spent a considerable time in the area, and Mr. Moshe Edelman (1982).

The first contact with Israel was made in 1981, when Mr. Victor Chico was chosen out of 300 contestants to represent Peru in the Bible competition in Jerusalem. He returned with many impressions that he shared with his people, and with recordings of Israeli songs.

During this time Joshua, son of Segundo, taught himself Hebrew with a Spanish-Hebrew dictionary, was sent to Lima to study the prayers and liturgy of the Sephardic Jewish Community, and quickly became the teacher of the group. In an attempt to enrich their awareness of Judaism, the men of the group made phylacteries, *mezuzot*, and a *Torah* scroll for their own use.

Amishav

Initial contact with the Amishav Organization was established on July 12, 1987, when a letter written by Mr. David Liss was brought to Amishav by Professor Chaim Avni. In the letter Mr. Liss wrote: "It will be a great *mitzvah* for Judaism if something is done for this group". Included with the letter were locally published articles about the group. Some months later, Mr. Gideon Tadmor spoke with Rabbi Avichail about the group, and initiated the contact with Amishav.

Mr. David Kuyperstock of Tel Aviv, originally from Peru, maintains commercial relations with Peru and established contact with the group in Lima in 1988. He also recommended assistance in conversion, and subsequently provided extensive assistance in the matter. In the summer of 1988, Amishav sent Mr. Jonathan Segal to meet the group and examine their knowledge and sincerity. He returned greatly excited by his findings, and became very active on behalf of the group.

Contact was then made with Rabbis Jacob Krauss and Abraham Ben Hamu of Lima, and upon their recommendations to the Chief Rabbinate of Israel, Amishav formed a Rabbinical Court to examine and convert deserving members of the group.

With the authorization of the Chief Rabbi of Israel Rabbi Mordechai Eliyahu, Amishav President Rabbi E. Avichail (the writer) traveled to Peru with Rabbi Mordechai Oriah, chief of the Haifa Rabbinical Court. Together with Rabbi Krauss, the Ashkenazi Rabbi of Lima, they set up a rabbinical court for conversion. Rabbi Kraus worked devotedly, despite difficulties and opposition from his own community. The Court converted 11 families of the group in the cities of Trujillo (Almilagro) and Lima, totaling 58 persons. On August 24, 1989, the Bnei Moshe converts underwent the prescribed ritual immersion in the Moche river near Trujillo, after which proper wedding ceremonies were performed for the married couples. The conversion of the Alvaro, Villanueva, and Salirosas families of Lima was similarly performed a week later in the sea near Lima.

About six months after the conversion, on February 28, 1990, after many years of dreaming and longing for Zion and Israel, the Bnei Moshe arrived in Israel, and were lovingly and joyously received by the people of the Elon Moreh settlement in Samaria, who had heard of them from Amishav and from Mr. Kuyperstok.

The group arrived in Israel with song, dance and prayer, a sight such as was never seen at Ben-Gurion Airport. They were received with song, dance and flowers by inhabitants of Elon Moreh, who had waited many hours until the bureaucratic steps were completed. After midnight the group reached Elon Moreh and the entire settlement came out to welcome the new immigrants in a moving reception. The absorption of the Bnei Moshe in Elon Moreh received wide media coverage and aroused extensive public interest in Israel and abroad. Since then the group has lived in Elon Moreh, where it has become a symbol of successful absorption of new immigrants in Israel.

Approximately one year later, additional families in Peru who were connected to the community were converted and joined their friends in Israel. Today the Bnei Moshe community in Elon Moreh numbers about 150. They have fulfilled their hopes of many years and are living completely as Jews in the Land of Israel.

THE "BAYUDAYA" OF UGANDA

Recently there has been a great awakening throughout Africa to Israel and Judaism. This is currently true in Nigeria (the Ibo tribe – fifteen million), in Cameroon (the Bassa tribe – about two million), southwest Ethiopia (the Gayon/Gihon(?) tribe – about 4 million), Zaire (about a million), Zimbabwe and Mozambique (the Lemba tribe), Somalia (Galjal – Yibir?), Ghana and in many other localities.

The motivation varies from one people to another. In many cases, the relation to Judaism is erroneous, embracing both the Bible and the New Testament. (There are also similar manifestations in Latin America.) Some claim a connection to the awakening and return of "Beta Israel" from Ethiopia, and claim that they are also part of this people. Some may be motivated by a desire to flee from persecution, poverty and poor economic conditions.

One of the first such "Jewish" groups sprang up in Uganda, already in the early twentieth century (1917), in the form of the "Bayudaya" community. Today its members are closer to full Jewish life than any of its fellow-groups in Africa.

Uganda

In the early nineteenth century widespread secession from the Christian Church in Uganda commenced, for various reasons: social, political, economic and even religious. In the rich kingdom of Buganda, one of the four kingdoms of Uganda, there is developed agriculture (coffee, cotton and banana crops), revealing a relatively good situation. One of the clans in this kingdom is the Ganda clan, belonging to the Bagisu and Bakedi tribes, living between the sources of the Nile at Lake Victoria and Mount Elgon close to the Kenyan border.

Semei Kakungulu was the talented chief of these tribes. Kakungulu was an important and central personage in all Uganda, and was greatly esteemed by the British rulers of the country. He was appointed District Chief in Buganda and military commander of the entire kingdom. He participated and triumphed in wars against the Moslems and Catholics at the end of the nineteenth century. He assisted the British in their conquest of Uganda. Disappointed by the British, he retired from military and political activity, and began to focus on religious activity. He also commenced his spiritual journey by way of the Bible.

The "Bayudaya"

From study of the book of Zechariah, Kakungulu concluded that he must find his way to the true faith through the Jews: "Thus says the Lord of hosts: In those days it shall come to pass that ten men shall take hold out of the languages of the nation, even shall take hold of the skirt of him that is a Jew, saying we will go with you: for we have heard that God is with you."[1] However, because of ignorance, he also saw the New Testament as part of the Bible (since it is bound together with the "Old Testament" in the Christian Bible). He founded the "Bayudaya" (which means "Jews" in the Lugandan language) in 1917.

In the ritual prayer book, at this early stage, there was a mixture of Christianity and the New Testament, together also with the "Old Testament". Kakungulu appointed paid teachers in all the area under his authority and declared himself a "Jew". Gradually they drew near to true Jewish practice. He set up a Jewish community in Gangama at the foot of Mount Elgon, where he lived for a few years.

In 1926 in Kampala, the Bugandan capital, he encountered Joseph, a dark-complexioned bearded Jew who became Kakungulu's teacher and friend. Joseph taught that the New Testament had no part in Judaism. He came to Kakungulu's town of Mbale and spent several weeks there teaching him. Kakungulu died in 1928, leaving a Jewish heritage to his followers in several of these villages, who continued to live as

1   Zachariah 8:23.

Jews without Christian influences. Today they number some 500, have synagogues and observe Jewish customs and prayers. Life in these villages is primitive, without electricity and running water, and homes lack all the comforts of modern civilization, but the people are honestly and truly devoted to their Jewish way of life.

Amishav

In 1992, the Association for Converts in Israel asked Amishav to help arrange the absorption of two youth from the Bayudaya so they could study in Israel and convert. The Association agreed to make arrangements for study but not to bring them to Israel. After contact with Rabbi Worsh of Melbourne, Australia, who had visited the Bayudaya and been greatly impressed by their sincerity, Amishav recommended sending a rabbi-teacher to teach the Bayudaya how to live full Jewish lives if they sincerely wish to convert and immigrate to Israel.

BA'DEREJ LEYERUSHALAIM
OF MEXICO

In Jalapa and Veracruz

In the cities of Jalapa, situated in the beautiful mountainous region only a 4-hour drive away from Mexico City, and Veracruz, located on the coast south of Mexico City, there was a group of about 200 people living Jewish lives in a community framework around the Veracruz synagogue. Some of these people had a tradition of being descendants of Marranos who had arrived from Spain. Others retained a few Jewish traditions and customs passed down from previous generations. The group was united by its wish to live full Jewish lives and to immigrate to Israel.

The community began to organize in 1982. They were unsuccessful in their attempts to be converted by Orthodox rabbis in Mexico, because of the opposition on principle to conversion that has existed in Mexico for the last forty years. Some of the community members succeeded in converting in the United States and Canada, and some converted recently through the Amishav Organization in Israel.

They lived Jewish lives for years before their conversion and immigration to Israel. The conversion process began by a meeting with the Amishav Organization in 1984, when the community's leader visited Israel with his wife and sought Amishav's help. They appealed to the Chief Rabbi of Israel, the Rishon Lezion, Rabbi Mordechai Eliyahu, who referred them to Amishav, saying that "It is a great *Mitzvah* to assist them." A rabbinical court was sent by Amishav to Mexico, headed by a presiding Israeli rabbi, and the community converted in several stages and immigrated to Israel.

Venta Prieta

In the town of Venta Prieta (approximately 80 km from Mexico City), there is a group of about 150 people who have been living as Jews for about 40 years. They have a synagogue, a cemetery, a mikveh and an attractive building for community activity, all of which they built themselves.

The community originated with a family descended from Spanish Marranos, many of whom had intermarried and assimilated with the local inhabitants. Over the years all returned to Judaism and came to live as Jews. Some of the community has undergone Orthodox conversion, and some non-Orthodox conversion. Some of their children have studied in religious institutes in Israel, and they speak Hebrew.

Rabbi Eliyahu Avichail is the Founder and Chairman of Amishav. Since 1961, he has dedicated his life to research and activity on behalf of the dispersed of Israel, in particular, research regarding the fate of the Ten Tribes. In 1975, at the urging of his rabbi, Rabbi Tzvi Yehuda Kook zt"l, he founded the non-profit organization "Amishav – for the Dispersed of Israel".

Rabbi Avichail has lectured widely in Israel and abroad, published numerous articles and the Hebrew books *HaAvudim B'Eretz Ashur* and *Shivtei Yisrael*, the latter of which has been translated into English and French. In order to assist in aliyah and conversion, he wrote and published the booklet *Judaism* (Hebrew) which has been translated into numerous languages.

Rabbi Avichail was a member of the Rabbinical Court which converted the Belmonte community in Portugal. He facilitated aliyah of the 'BaDerej L'Yerushalayim' group from Mexico and the 'Bnei Moshe' group from Peru. The continues to assist the *aliyah* of Bnei Menashe from northeast India (some 1,000 souls to date). Rabbi Avichail has travelled the world from India, Burma, China, Thailand and Japan to Europe and South America in order to research, encourage and guide the dispersed of Israel.

Rabbi Avichail was born in Jerusalem in 1932. His parents camefrom Lithuania and the Ukraine. At 16, he was drafted by the Israel Defense Forces during the War of Independence; he completed his service with the rank of sergeant in the 'Nahal' brigade at Kibbutz Yavneh.

After wards, he joined Kibbutz Saad where he lived and worked for five years study at Kerem beYavneh and Mercaz HaRav Kook. He received his rabbinical ordination through completed a teaching certificate for Tanach and Mishna. He has held the positions of community rabbi, students' rabbi at the Hebrew University, teacher of Bible end Judaism at all ages.

He received the equivalent of a Doctorate in Jewish Professions for his rabbinical studies and publications.

Rabbi Avichail and Rivka have six children, thirty two grandchildren and two great-grandchildren. Their home is open at all times to the Bnei Menashe, new convert and all who to study Judaism.

Amishav2012@gmail.com

Made in United States
North Haven, CT
25 March 2025

67229193R00130